THE FORMULA

Transforming a Failing School in One of the Nation's Deadliest Zip Codes from War Zone to Winning Institution in One Year

KHALILAH CAMPBELL-RHONE, Ed.D.

The Formula: Transforming a Failing School in One of the Nation's
Deadliest Zip Codes from War Zone to Winning Institution in One Year

Copyright © 2022 by Khalilah Campbell-Rhone

Printed in the United States of America

For permissions, bulk orders, or bookings, please address correspondence
to: TheEducationalFormula@gmail.com

ISBN: 978-1-7378085-0-3

Table of Contents

Dedication

To my husband, Stanley, and Stanley II, Sidney and Kaylani.

In Loving Memory of
Jessica Broom, who taught me the true meaning
of what loving beyond the books meant. 1987 – 2021

My Daddy. I didn't think I could do it without you,
but, even in spirit, you led me here. 1937- 2011

Acknowledgements

There is not enough time or paper in all the world for me to acknowledge everyone that was the stimulus for this book or the cheerleader for its completion.

First, there are those who have passed on from this life but who remain in my heart, providing constant inspiration for me, both in life and in the writing of this book. Thank you to my Daddy (1937- 2011), who continues to lead and guide me to the places I need to go, even when I am afraid to go there. You give me the confidence and courage I need.

I also hold the memory of Jessica Broom (1987 – 2021) close to my heart. Jessica taught me the true meaning of what loving beyond the books meant. She was a student in the first class I ever taught. We stayed in contact and she became a substitute teacher where I was principal. I watched her grow and mature, and I could not have been prouder of her accomplishments in such a short time on this side of the earth. Just as much as I ever taught her, she taught me more in return. Teaching, leading and mentorships matter – tremendously. Rest well, Jessica.

Next, I am deeply grateful to my family. To my husband, Stanley, thank you for your belief in me and your support. Nothing comes easily for us, but eventually, it always comes. Love you for life, and then a few more days.

Thank you, Stanley II, Sidney and Kaylani for giving me space to write (okay, sometimes - it usually happened after you were long gone to sleep, but your inquisitiveness about when I would *finally be done'* helped push the work along). Thank you for allowing Mommy to do the work that I have done! I pray that my efforts have and will continue to have a first-hand impact on the way you navigate the world. I hope that your view of education and its importance remain with you as you traverse life. Remember: always help someone accomplish their goals to be a better human as you continually better yourselves. Never forget to say, "Please" and "Thank you!" and always, *always* help your elders.

Mom, you are my rock. I couldn't imagine life without you. Thank you for giving me the opportunity to save others' children as you make sure my own are saved. Our lives are whole because of you.

To my Mother in Love, Ellen, thank for completing our village. Your consistency offered an additional layer of support to the family, and we are forever grateful. Nancy, Harvey and Caleb, thank you for the love and support!

To my two brothers, Kassem and Micheal, and their wives, Jessica and Kelly, thank you for playing such a huge role in my life and my life as an educator. Because we do everything as a family, so many times, you are dragged into helping me solve problems, with projects and events - and you do it with love. Our late night conversations shape who I am and what I do. Love you all for that!

To my niece Ryann, who is now a teacher and was awarded "New Teacher of the Year" for her school this year. I am immensely proud of you. To Sydney and Micheal, I watch you proudly as you continue to grow. Know that Aunt Kha will always be your biggest fan!

I would be remiss if I didn't acknowledge the many teachers, staff, school support officers and police officers at all of the campuses I have led for their tireless work to ensure the achievement of students academically, and equally as important, personally.

Your willingness to get 'in the work' and to have amazing rapport with students has changed the trajectory for more students than we'll ever be able to surmise. You are the reason that turnaround work has been possible at all the campuses where I have served in leadership!

To the one person who read through the book more times than I: Lauren Harris. You gave me vision on the nights when I had none. Your 2 AM consistency awakened my excitement in the wee hours of the morning. Your memory is impeccable! Your Dad is proud!

To Monica, Carolyn and CaSandra, can we *please* take our trip now? B. Ward, grab the mic – Let's talk about this!

To all of my fellow principals, we are and will forever be linked by our desire to do what is best for the kids and the community we serve. No one will understand loving other people's children as though they are your own – and being willing to go miles for their success. Thank you for the silent pushes, the sharing of information and the competition! This is what we do.

To any educator who desires to make immense change in the lives of students, particularly those who have been underserved or underprivileged, you can be the impetus for that change!

To everyone I have mentioned and anyone I might have missed, please know that I appreciate you greatly! From the early morning phone calls to the late-night text messages and every word of encouragement, from the bottom of my heart, THANK YOU!

> "The precipitous decline of [this campus], home to about 850 students, illustrates how a toxic combination of ineffective leadership and teachers, inequitable education policies and intergenerational poverty can ravage an urban neighborhood school, leaving children uneducated and unprepared to enter the workforce.
>
> - Jacob Carpenter, *Houston Chronicle*, Sunday, July 15, 2018

INTRODUCTION
A Picture Is Worth a Thousand Words... or Is It?

We are all familiar with the adage, "A picture is worth a thousand words." However, when *Houston Chronicle* readers saw the photo of my team and me, dressed in all black, during a press conference announcing that our Houston area high school had successfully met state standards in only one year and could keep the doors open – something no one thought was possible – they thought our matching attire was simply a display of unity and strength. No one had any inkling about the *real* story, the actual meaning behind dressing in black, behind the picture that would soon become front page news.

You see, from the time I was selected to become the principal of the school in spring 2017, it was a commonly accepted "fact" that I was fighting a losing battle. The school, a cornerstone in Houston's predominately black neighborhood of Sunnyside, having an unemployment rate of 29% in 2016 (the highest percentage of any community in Houston) while the city's overall unemployment rate was 5.5%, was the only high school to have the fate of the district riding on its back. If we didn't improve in one year, we'd be closed, or trigger a state takeover of the entire district because of a state law known as HB1842. The school had been failing to meet consistent state standards for nearly a decade and had gone through numerous principals over the past several years. In fact, the school was considered so far beyond transformation that if we didn't improve and improve fast, we were slated to be closed down. Forever.

Many believed that appointing me as the principal was merely a formality – the "right thing to do," if you will. They didn't really expect me to be able to make a difference, especially within the time constraints. Most figured I was put into the principalship of a losing school, like a coach plugs his bench-warming players into a game when the team is losing by 50 points, with two minutes before the final buzzer. Some said, "Well, if the school is going to close its doors anyway, why not give her a shot?" The mere thought that both my passion and determination were underestimated tickled me. My commitment to seeing students receive their rightful entitlement, which was a quality education, regardless of their race or class, was overlooked. Most of all, they underestimated my will to win.

With a stringent, one-year timeline, my hand-picked team (many former employees abandoned the call to action or believed that there would be no more school, but I'll talk about this later in the book) and I took drastic action to turn around the most vital institution in Houston's Sunnyside community. We put in the work to change the culture, foster a new climate of hope among students and teachers, decrease the dropout rate while increasing test scores and graduation rates, morale, and students' beliefs that they could achieve more and go further in life than their sometimes violent, many times neglected, and impoverished surroundings suggested they could. We worked early mornings, late nights, weekends, and holidays to get our students caught up academically so that they would be successful on the end-of-course exams by which our fitness to continue to function as a school would ultimately be judged. We withstood the constant scrutiny from outsiders and frequent visits from state and district level employees who were assigned to our campus for the purpose of ensuring that we were carrying out the turnaround plan we'd put into place to transform the school. We did everything humanly possible to help the school meet the state's standards of accountability within the given timeline so that the school would not have to close its doors and re-open as another school in the future.

At the end of the year, when it was time for the Texas Education Agency to make its final ruling on the fate of the school, my team hoped that all of the efforts we'd engaged in, and sacrifices we'd made for the sake of our kids, would be enough (honestly, more than enough) to keep the doors of the school open. Our students were tested, and we waited for the results, our hopes and expectations high. Prior to the state releasing their final numbers, we had district projections. All numbers pointed to the school scarcely missing the mark. We were devastated. We were stunned to receive the most disappointing news of our careers: our testing results were not projected to meet state standards. This school, one of the most beloved and most prominent institutions in the Sunnyside community, and one of the most legendary and well-known high schools in the greater Houston community, would not survive to see another year.

As my team and I reflected on all that we had done to avoid such a disappointing outcome, there were many tears shed behind closed doors. Our only comfort was knowing that we'd done everything a school staff could possibly do in order to help our students succeed. The school's closure was simply fate. We pledged to keep the information to ourselves and announce the news of the crushing defeat via a press conference our district scheduled for the following Wednesday.

As the day neared, we knew it would be a day of mourning the imminent closing of our school. We agreed that we would all wear black for the press conference. Each of us grieved intensely over the entire weekend. In our group text, we lamented about how unfair it was that we worked hard and smart, invested all our time, effort, and energy; yet we still missed the mark. We questioned where we went wrong and vowed to go back to the drawing board and get better at everything we knew! It was one of the hardest, most painful, longest weekends that any of us had ever experienced in our professional careers. If there was one thing synonymous with our team, it was that we all hated to lose!

On August 15, 2018, we showed up on campus, dressed in all black, just as we'd agreed. We busied ourselves in advance of the press conference, which was to occur at 10:00 AM. That day, the final scores would arrive. I went into my office to check my e-mail. Since I was alone for the moment, I decided to log into the Texas Education Agency site, where the scores were posted, to witness the damage and grieve my failure privately. There they were: the final results of our state testing. I braced myself for the finality of the news that I was about to read and clicked to open it. What I saw on my computer screen caused me to pause. *We MET accountability?* This couldn't be right. I checked it again. And again. The official report said that we'd met accountability standards! Not wanting to celebrate prematurely, I ran out of my office and called in my assistant principals to verify that I was seeing what I thought I was seeing. They rushed into my office and glared closely at the computer screen. As each of their eyes rested on the words announcing the results, there were screams. We could not believe our eyes! There, in my office, we cheered, hugged, and cried tears of pure, authentic, and unrehearsed happiness. Everyone celebrated differently, but joyously! I hurried myself to collect my thoughts and prepare my statement for an altogether different press conference than I had planned. I couldn't wait to announce the news to the world. There at the press conference, we stood behind the podium in all black, and the newspaper photographer took our picture. I'm sure that people who saw it in the newspaper thought, *Oh, that's nice. The school's leadership team is so unified, wearing all black as a show of unity to celebrate their success.* Well, they didn't know the half of it!

What we thought was the biggest and most devastating blow of all of our careers, turned out to be the beginning of one of the biggest wins for kids and the Sunnyside community! In only one year, we were able to successfully lead the complete turnaround of a school that had been considered beyond transformation and slated for closure. Along the way, as a team, we hired a new staff, significantly increased graduation rates, changed students' trajectory by ensuring they were preparing for college, drastically reduced attrition rates, and even received an early college designation, which allowed our kids to take college courses while in high school and earn an associate degree upon graduation.

As soon as the news that our high school would remain open hit the media, word spread like wildfire around the city of Houston, the state of Texas, and around the United States. The story of beating all odds flooded social media and was the topic of conversation in state educational agencies, major school districts around the nation, as well as educational conferences. However, the conversation was not just about the success story itself; it was about the potentials that the story spoke to concerning the ability of persistently failing schools to be turned around, and about the significant role of transformational leadership when approaching such efforts. The story carried a significant implication: the reason that schools in underserved areas fail is because of leadership. With the right leader at the helm, schools in impoverished, neglected or violent communities can excel, despite their surroundings and limited resources.

Following these conversations, the same questions were always asked: who led the change, and how did she do it? This was the question to which everyone wanted the answer. I understood why people asked. Over the past 10 years, equally talented former administrations were unsuccessful. What was the difference? What was *The Formula*? I have finally been able to take a long enough break to recover and reflect. You know the what, as well as the why. Now, I am ready to share with you my how: *The Formula* that pushed us past ordinary.

I've written this book for two audiences, for two distinct purposes. First, I've written to the thousands of Houstonians, both members of the community and supporters, who love our school and simply want to know how we managed to deliver such a big win to this historic school. They want the behind-the-scenes story, and in the pages of this book, I deliver just that: the story. You'll find it to be simultaneously entertaining, heartbreaking, and inspirational.

Second, I've written to the millions of educators in the United States, from aspiring and active public and private school teachers, to principals, assistant principals, school district officers, school board members, and anyone else who is vested in delivering quality education to students in underserved populations, particularly those tasked with turning around underperforming schools. If this is you, whether you are assigned this book to read as a college student studying education, asked to read this book in a teacher training or licensure program, requested to secure and review a copy of this book as an administrator, or using this book for any other training or developmental purposes, I guarantee that you'll learn some valuable lessons about operating as a transformational leader.

Sure, you'll get the story of *what* I did, but most importantly, you'll also learn *how* I integrated the principles of transformational leadership into the work!

The Formula is intended to help leaders identify, grasp, own, and execute their vision for transformation. Often, people may glorify a leadership position, not knowing the purpose, commitment, and sacrifice behind the position. However, as a leader, it is critical to understand the "why" behind the work that you do and to have the heart to do it. For this reason, at the conclusion of each chapter, you will be provided with essential **Transformational Leadership Tips (TLTs)** to add to your leadership toolbox. TLTs are principles of transformational leadership meant to be used as a compass to guide leaders and their teams through the process of shifting their lens, practice, and thinking, specifically in turnaround spaces.

It is my sincere desire that as you allow me to recount the story of our school's transformation, your beliefs about the difference that one person – a dedicated, passionate, transformational leader with an *amazing* team – can make in record time will inspire you to become a transformational change agent in your own context.

1
Transformational Leadership

Leading through Inspiration, Motivation, & Relationship

Just in case you're not familiar with the transformational leadership style, allow me to give you a primer. Originally introduced by James MacGregor Burns (1978) in his research on leadership in the political arena, transformational leadership has become adapted as an effective style of leadership in nearly every industry. Transformational leadership is a style of leadership driven by a set of soft skills; leaders lead followers through encouragement, inspiration, and motivation for the purpose of creating change and innovation, resulting in the organization's success.[1] After all, an organization is not a physical facility or a fixed structure; an organization is a group of people working toward a common cause. If you're going to change an organization, you must have the ability, bandwidth, and grit to transform the people. Transformational leaders focus on transforming people in order to turn around organizations while increasing organizational productivity, profitability, and effectiveness.

The concept of transformational leadership is best understood in contrast to the concept of transactional leadership. At its simplest level, transactional leadership is about a paycheck for work performed. It's simply a transaction: you give me this, and I give you that. Transactional leadership is void of care, concern, or investment into the follower. Transactional leaders tend to practice contingent reinforcement to motivate those who work for them—motivating employees through punishments for undesirable behavior and rewards for desirable behavior.[2]

In transactional leadership, the leader-follower relationship tends to be a shallow one, because it is simply about an exchange: the leader communicates what the follower is to do (actively or passively) in order to receive a reward and avoid undesirable consequences like corrective action.[3] This produces a work climate in which the follower is motivated by not failing rather than being motivated to make every effort to succeed and excel at the work. As a result, followers are not compelled to give the organization their best. They simply do what they have to do in order to keep their job. Nothing more.

In contrast to the cold and relationally-distant leader-follower exchange style of transactional leadership, transformational leaders operate with a warmer, more personalized and invested approach. They place an emphasis on their followers' intrinsic motivation: they seek to understand what drives each follower individually and they appeal to it in order to influence them towards greater levels of commitment and buy-in to the organization, and its mission. Rather than trying to force followers into compliance based on rewards and punishments, they lead followers into sincerely and organically wanting to do what the organization needs them to do, helping them to see that doing so is in their own best interest.

Transformational leaders seek to positively develop their followers through inspiration, motivation, morale, and giving them a higher sense of purpose when approaching the work that they are doing.[4] They don't just give them a task list to complete and a deadline by which to complete it. Instead, they help their followers to see how their individual tasks, roles, and responsibilities tie into the bigger picture of what the organization is trying to accomplish—its mission. I like the example that Jeffrey Shipley, Vice President and CIO at Blue Cross and Blue Shield of Kansas City, provided as an illustrative example of this concept:

Two guys are digging a ditch. I asked one of them, "What are you doing?" He says, "Digging a ditch. What's it look like I'm doing?" I asked the other guy the same question, and he says, "I'm building a hospital."[5] Thus, when followers are carrying out their respective duties, transformational leaders help them to see themselves as making a valuable contribution to something larger, significant, and meaningful.

Transformational leaders utilize characteristics like charisma, inspiration, motivation, individualized care and concern, and intellectual stimulation to develop their followers' ideals. Their goal is to transform their followers' desires so that followers will want to achieve great goals for the organization, to reach their highest potential so that they can serve the organization better, and to increase their commitment to bettering the well-being of others.[6] As a result of the training, development, and mentorship that transformational leaders provide for their followers, an organizational culture characterized by creativity, innovation, independence, and agility results.[7]

Transformational leaders lead their followers in embracing what is best for the organization and what will advance their organization's mission over and above what is best for their own lives, personally. These leaders lead their followers into subjecting their own personal interests so that they can prioritize the values and interests of the organization. They help to tie their followers' sense of self-worth to being committed to and involved in every effort necessary to bring the organization's mission to pass.[8] At the same time, however, these leaders observe and identify areas where their followers need to be brought up to speed and then help their followers to grow and develop their own leadership capacity, which benefits both the follower and the organization.[9]

> The transformational leader emphasizes what you can do for your country; the transactional leader, on what your country can do for you.[10]

In case you haven't picked up on it yet, I consider myself a transformational leader. As you read about my story and style of leadership in the chapters to come, you will see example after example of transformational leadership in action. When I accepted the position as principal of this Houston area high school, I knew that in order to transform the failing organization, I had to transform the *people*. Further, I knew that I couldn't accomplish this through the traditional style of rewards and reprimands: you do what I say or you're out of here! Instead, my work was focused on inspiring, motivating, and compelling my administrative team, faculty, and staff members. It was about helping them truly and authentically buy into the mission of helping our kids achieve state standards so we could keep the school's doors open, as well as identifying where each of my team members needed to be developed individually and developing them in those areas. It took mentoring and selling the big picture. It was all about leading the team to a point where they sacrificed their time, their resources, their comfort, their convenience, their evenings and weekends, and sometimes time with their families, prioritizing the interests of the organization over their own interests. It was also about making them feel good about doing so. As a result, the school experienced unprecedented transformation in record time, and our story will forever be engrained in the fabric of the community, city, and state.

It is my goal to help you, the reader, understand the methods and mentalities that I engaged in as a transformational leader in the education arena. Of course, there are not enough hours in the day to write about all that happened! However, I thought it was important to share a small glimpse into how I functioned as a transformational leader in order to introduce how I was able to effectively employ this leadership style and successfully turn around a failing school.

What Does It Take to Be an Effective Transformational Leader in Education?

Before I share my story about how I used a transformational leadership style to turn around a failing school, allow me to share a few keys that will help you maximize your own success as a transformational leader.

Transformational Leadership Key 1: Be Willing to Put in the Work

Although I've been part of and led the change at several schools, my most recent and most challenging experience has finally allowed me to put my experience into words! For years, I couldn't quite put my finger on what the most important leadership key was. I often wondered if it was about my ability to build relationships and offer high accountability. Was it about the curriculum and who delivered it? What was the one particular key for transforming organizations? While all aspects are significant, I have found the one that is paramount. If you're going to be successful as a transformational leader, you've got to be willing to put in the work yourself.

Hard work is undeniably not for the faint of heart. As a young girl, my parents, Leroy and Beverly Campbell, instilled that value in me, and I've carried it with me my entire life. Some may identify hard work as putting a great deal of effort into a physical task. I'm here to tell you, the work is not always physical. Imagine being pushed beyond your mental limit and capacity. Now, fathom being pushed even further than what you conceived you could possibly go. That's the type of hard work I'm speaking of. There will be days where you make what feels like more than one hundred decisions within an hour, have multiple face-to-face, virtual, and phone conversations, walk classrooms until your feet throb in utter agony, and your body feels as if it has just completed a triathlon. But guess what? The race is nowhere near over, because you are still swimming, pushing yourself to the next phase of that mental race.

Total transformation and turnaround of an organization is something that you hear happening more in business than in education, but it actually *does* happen in education. However, I personally believe that the reason we don't see it happening as much in education is because many leaders are not prepared to put in the work! I like to often quip that, "We make this look easy!" When in fact, it's the complete opposite. A lot of educators get into the field because they want something stable and predictable. They have this vision of, "I'm going to go to work at this time, I'm going to get off at that time, I'm going to have these days off…" Be warned: this is *not* the life of a transformational leader in education.

Transformational leaders internalize the organizational mission and carry it around with them 24 hours a day. Even when they aren't at work, they are thinking, analyzing, processing, strategizing, and planning. They are so driven to execute the mission, increase productivity and turn things around, that their mind never settles. The organization, and most of all, the *people* within the organization, are always at the top of their mind. Anyone who has been around me knows that this is the way I operate. I lived and breathed the school's transformation, because I wanted to give our kids all that they deserved. As a result, I'd get ideas at one o'clock in the morning, and to ensure I wouldn't forget them, I'd jump out of bed, quickly jotting them down to act on them the next day. Later, I got smarter and started whispering to Siri to open my notes in my phone in the wee hours of the morning. Yes, I could have slept through some of those thoughts and ideas, but true transformational leaders must always stay focused on the *urgency* of transformation. We don't see ourselves as driving a slow-moving tugboat. Instead, we see ourselves as steering a speedboat, during a hurricane, running low on gas. We know that time is limited. We know that we must get to safety. We know that lives depend on us. We also know that we'll look up, and the year will be over. So, we move quickly and with great agility.

When you think of what it takes to lead change in a turnaround environment, you have to think about the environment of the school, the culture, the master schedule, the bell schedule, the work orders for items in the building needing repair, feeding hungry students, getting clothes to those in need, making sure that kids arrive on time, grading cycles, washing clothes for students without access to water, vetting curriculum, providing hygiene products, making sure social and emotional needs are met, clearing halls, hiring certified teachers, monitoring teacher capacity, meeting with parents, completing teacher walk-throughs, and providing relevant professional development with the expectation it will be implemented by teachers and staff immediately. Did I happen to mention this is all before breakfast?

You must be willing to prioritize events, conversations, text messages, and emails, all while maintaining a laser-like focus on moving the needle, guaranteeing the school is not on fire, students are safe, and your commitment to your own family remains at the forefront. With great responsibility comes great accountability.

Transformational Leadership Key 2: Sharpen Your Ability to See What's Lacking

One of the most critical skills of a transformational leader is the ability to walk into an environment, assess it to determine what's lacking, then map out a needs assessment, identifying how those needs will be executed (or implemented), and what the execution (or implementation) process will look like. Although I've earned my bachelor's, master's, and doctoral degrees, all in the area of education, this is not a skill that most leaders, including myself, learn in school. This education alone did not equip me with the skills I needed to see what a failing school organization needed, and what was necessary to turn it around. Instead, I would say that my classroom preparation only gave me a *foundation* to be able to go into and assess an environment in order to make radical change as a transformational leader.

My ability to assess an environment to determine what is lacking is more of a skill set that I developed over the course of my career, and I purposely did so. It happened through a combination of exercising care, concern, and critically thinking through processes. It helps me to discern how things are operating not only at surface level, but underneath the surface and behind the scenes. Peeling the onion, if you will. This skill set allows me to walk into a situation, observe what's good and actually working (not what merely appears to be working), what's bad and not working, and what needs help, on a more granular level. It also helps me to develop a plan for how to get these things working properly, assess the outcomes of the plan in action, and make continual adjustments, as necessary. If you can develop this valuable skill set of being able to identify what's lacking in an organization and what specifically needs to be turned around, you will find it invaluable to your ability to function as a transformational leader.

Transformational Leadership Key 3: Lead Out of Relationships

Transformational leaders do not focus on leveraging pay for performance; they focus on leveraging strong relationships to get things done in the organization to drive the mission forward. While it is true that the people who work for you have to pay bills (which means that the paycheck *does* matter), there is another truth at work that should not be ignored: people work really hard for you because they like you as a leader. People do not give you high performance on the job because of a paycheck; this is what drives transactional leadership. Instead, if you are a transformational leader, people give you high performance on the job because they have a relationship with you, the leader, and they feel a sense of intrinsic value and pride in giving you what you've requested of them.

If you're going to be an effective transformational leader, you can't operate out of an authoritarian position. I think this is a critical piece that a lot of principals miss. They function out of a position of authority. "You do what I say because I said, 'Do it!' I'm the boss!" It's not always about setting the rules and issuing memos when these rules are violated. Often, when rule violations occur, the first thing a leader will do is issue a reprimand. They say, "You're not doing what I asked you to do? I'm going to write you up!" Then, they eventually lose that person. When they lose the worker, the organization also loses, because now there's no continuity, and the stability of the environment is impacted. Continuity and stability are both very important to kids in a school environment. Does this mean you allow anyone in the organization to continuously operate in mediocrity? ABSOLUTELY NOT!

What it translates to is that transformational leaders are intentional about not always approaching things from the position of, "I'm going to get rid of this person and get somebody else if they don't do what I say do." Well, yes, you could do this, but the energy you put into terminating, interviewing, hiring, and so on, can be placed into strategically developing the very employee you considered terminating. Before you determine your next best step, you must ask yourself the following questions: Did I set clear expectations for this employee? Have I provided all the necessary resources for this person to be successful? Have I provided training for them? If the answer is yes to the aforementioned questions, then before lowering the axe, ask yourself one final question: Am I getting my biggest bang for my buck by pushing this person toward the exit?

For example, you might have a clerk who often comes in late. You call her in for excessive tardiness, and she immediately begins tearing up. You do some probing and discover that she's late because she's dropping her young kids, aged 2 and 4, off at the local daycare in Houston traffic. However, she's also willing to stay late to make up for the time that she misses in the morning, and besides that, she's a super hard worker, and very good at what she does. An authoritarian leader would fire her. As a transformational leader, you would offer care and concern, and work with her to produce a win-win for the organization. Her willingness to stay late ensures that your phones are covered in the evening. Making decisions with care, concern, and a sense of fairness mixed into the relationship equation, rather than just on the written rule alone, makes all the difference. Operating out of this transformational leadership trait also benefits the organization. Because these individuals know that they are sincerely cared for rather than treated like replaceable figures on an organization chart, they will give 120 percent, go the extra mile, and sacrifice everything they possibly can to deliver what I ask. The best part of it all is that when you have people like this around you, and you're keeping them happy, morale will be through the roof, and they'll affect change **beyond** belief.

Another benefit of building relationships with people and showing that you care for them is that you develop followers who will follow you virtually anywhere. When I mentor, develop, and invest in growing people, as transformational leaders do, they become my key players, and I want to keep them in the environment working with me. The best part is that because I develop these types of relationships with them, they want to stay around. For example, I had an *amazing* math teacher at the school. I kept him happy at all costs because I didn't want him to go anywhere. This was not just something that I thought to myself; I told him this often, because I wanted him to know that I saw him, valued him and his skill, and wanted him around. I also told him, "I want you working with me, but if you're offered a promotion, and you really want to go, just give me enough time to find somebody who is as good as you!" Guess what? He's obliged for 12 years now. From campus to campus, he's come with me. He is coveted by many principals, in multiple districts, across Texas. I say all of that to say, he's had many opportunities to leave, but he's chosen to stay with me, because he knows he is valued. I had a few English teachers like that. I had a few science teachers like that. Now that I think about it, I had *lots* of teachers like that! I've built relationships so strong with them, characterized by care, concern, support, development, inspiration, and more, that even though they have opportunities to make a lateral move, or sometimes even a promotion, they've chosen to stay in place. This is a classic outcome of effective transformational leadership.

Transformational Leadership Key 4: Provide Support

It's no secret that on a campus like ours, teachers had to work *extremely* hard. I took every opportunity I could to remind my teachers that they have to show up prepared to give 110 percent every single day. That every time our kids leave, they are depleted of what we have poured into them the day before. Thus, it was up to us to fill their cups daily. That can be taxing! Imagine having to simultaneously service 30 customers every hour on the hour, meeting 100 percent of their needs, with specificity (and most of their expectations), every single day. However, I told them that I'm willing to do whatever I can do to get them to that point, because that's my job. Remember: developing and supporting followers is a large part of the work of the transformational leader. Teachers are in front of our kids for 90 minutes at a time, four times a day, which means they directly impact the majority of the kids in that grade level. If they're not happy, if they don't come in at 110 percent, or if they don't feel equipped, like they are serving any real purpose, they will negatively impact all of the students that they stand before in the classroom. As a transformational leader, my job is to make sure that whatever I can do to give them the proper amount of support, I do just that. And beyond. I wanted my teachers to know we have a relationship, and that I'm there for them.

Transformational leaders immerse themselves in the organization and get down into the trenches with their followers. Nothing is considered "too lowly" of a function for me to do in order to provide support for my followers as the leader of the school. I'm in the work, all the time, and my teachers and team members know this. I'm in it with them. I'm planning with them. I'm talking to them about what's happening. I made it my business to know the kids so we can be on the same page when we talk about them. When teachers tell me that a particular kid was standing up and talking in the middle of class, I'll say, "Yeah, you're right. That's what he always does. Okay, now what are we going to do differently for that kid, because we know that's what he's going to do every day?" Then, we work together—leader and follower—to come up with a solution that helps both the teacher and the student succeed.

If a teacher was having a difficult time, not following certain processes, or not getting the desired results in the classroom, rather than a reprimand being my first resort, as a transformational leader, I offer the teacher support. Sometimes you have to step back and say, "Okay, she's doing all of this in a classroom with 25 kids. What can I do to offer support to her in this area? What can I do to alleviate the stress that this teacher is under? Have I complimented and highlighted her small wins? Have I ensured the discipline referrals she sent in are taken care of? Are her classroom numbers excessive? Are all of the troublemakers in the same class?" Taking this step back and offering support, guidance, care, and concern is the difference between the way some principals lead, and those who operate with a transformational leadership style, banking big wins.

Transformational Leadership Key 5: Embrace a Life of Challenge

Transformational leaders tend to like challenges. Why else would someone choose to willingly go into an unproductive or failing organization and put their abilities to the test to turn that organization around? As you prepare to function as a transformational leader in education, you should approach opportunities with the realistic expectation that you're conquering a challenge. If you're going to be an effective transformational leader, you've got to thrive on challenges!

Early on in my educational career, I started out wanting to work with the most challenged kids in the school district. Over time, however, I grew to a point where I said, "You know, I've got my own kids now. I really want to go home at a decent hour and enjoy my own family." This lasted for a short season, as I soon realized this wasn't my niche. Working in "easy" opportunities in education was not where I blossomed; they didn't represent what I was best at doing. I realized that I'm good at "fixing" things, and I was at my best when I was taking on the challenge of turning the impossible to possible. This was where I thrived! I had to finally get comfortable with this reality. I had to face the fact that I would probably never operate in an environment where everything was going to be operating as it should. I get bored too quickly in places like that. I want to jump in, make changes for the better, and fix things. I enjoy a good challenge, because challenges have pushed me to grow into the transformational leader that I am today.

At this point in life, I'm very comfortable with the kind of transformational, turnaround situations I've been in, because they wake me up in the morning, giving me a sense of purpose. I know that once I get out of bed and place my feet on the ground, I'm going to be running until the end of the day. There's no, "Today's going to be a slow day," or "Today's going to be an easy day" in the forecast. Instead, every day is going to bring a different type of excitement, a different type of joy, and a different type of win. Every day is going to be an adventure-filled challenge, and as a transformational leader, I love it!

Transformational Leadership Key 6: Keep Focused on the Mission

When you enter into an environment that needs to be transformed, you're certain to be surrounded by all kinds of things that can distract you from the core mission: turning around the organization. Therefore, if you are going to be effective as a transformational leader, you have to master the ability to focus on the mission, despite all of the other things around you that are crying out for your focus and attention.

This was the case with me when I became the principal of the high school. The things that I *could* have addressed were limitless.

There was always something that felt pressing. There were emails, meetings that could have been emails, unexpected visitors, and sometimes, angry parents that had to be assuaged. However, I was there to accomplish one mission, and one mission alone: keep the doors of the school open by helping my students meet state testing accountability standards. There were some significant derailments that could have occurred if I hadn't remained focused on accomplishing this mission. If I hadn't stayed focused on this mission, there wouldn't be a school nearby in the community that the students could attend, and they would be transferred to other schools. If I hadn't stayed focused on this mission, this forgotten and underserved community, of which the school is an iconic mainstay, would have just been decimated. I think knowing that I wasn't just affecting the 900 kids that came to school, but that my focus on the mission would affect each home in and around the neighborhood, helped me to maintain an even greater focus on the mission, giving everything I had to drive it forward.

**

Being a transformational leader is challenging, difficult, and tiring work, but such challenges pale in comparison to the rewards. With all that is required of you as a transformational leader, you might feel defeated at the end of the day. However, at just the right time, a kid says, "Hey! I just wanted you to know I'm so thankful that x, y, z happened. It helped me a lot, and I really appreciate you!" All of a sudden, a big smile consumes your face, and you're filled with new energy! I even have kids texting me from the previous school year who don't even go to the school anymore with messages like, "I just wanted to tell you that you did an awesome job with us. I know sometimes we were bad, and I know sometimes you were frustrated, but in the end, we all won!" Somehow, these kids always know what to say to remind you that the hard work and sacrifices you put in as a transformational leader have made a difference. Then, just like that, you can't wait to go back to work again!

Chapter 1
Transformational Leadership Tips

What is Transformational Leadership?

- Transformational leadership starts from within. Your unique skill set will effectively shift an organization, propelling it to increased efficiency and success.

- Always consider your staff's needs, strengths and what factors motivate them. Knowing these key points will drive their commitment for the overall mission and vision.

- Continuously encourage, stimulate and motivate your staff, as you are building capacity within them to lead the work, thus pushing them to reach their highest potential.

TLT 1.1
Transformational Leadership Key 1:
Be Willing to Put in the Work

- Have expectations for yourself when it comes to leading and transforming an organization. The urgency you exhibit will be adopted by your staff.

- Hard work is expected, and it all comes down to how balanced you are at using your full capacity, mentally and physically, to reach your goal – all while maintaining your health and family time.

TLT 1.2
Transformational Leadership Key 2:
Sharpen Your Ability to See What's Lacking

- Create a needs assessment for the organization you are turning around. This will serve as your blueprint to drive the change. Once you've identified and prioritized those needs, you will be able to effectively begin the execution process.

TLT 1.3
Transformational Leadership Key 3:
Lead Out of Relationships

- Building solid, genuine relationships with your staff will afford you the ability to demand top performance from them. This will allow you to concentrate your energy on matters that need the most focus.

TLT 1.4
Transformational Leadership Key 4: Provide Support

- Your job is not only to lead, but to motivate your staff, provide support (job/personal) and show them that you care, all while leading.

TLT 1.5
Transformational Leadership Key 5:
Embrace a Life of Challenge

- Challenges will be inevitable. Know how to embrace them, confronting them head on with a solid plan of action to turn the organization around.

TLT 1.6
Transformational Leadership Key 6:
Keep Focused on the Mission

- Decide, understand and know the organization's mission indefinitely. This will determine how you will allocate your time to certain matters.

2
A Track Record of Turnaround Wins

Building My Brand as a Transformational Leader

When I entered the University of Houston in the fall of 1994, I was determined to become a pharmaceutical engineer. I'd prepared myself to tackle difficult science and math classes and readied myself to buckle down for the five years it would take me to complete the Pharm.D. program – a doctorate in pharmacy. What I didn't prepare myself for was the cost of college. In order to keep my scholarship, I had to participate in a work-study where we tutored at local middle schools. With my best friends, CC and Monica, in tow, we drove from the university to the local middle school three times per week.

While we were serving as tutors at the schools, we made a disturbing discovery: the students were far behind the benchmarks they should have been hitting at their grade level. They were nowhere near prepared to handle the level of work that awaited them in high school. I believe what disturbed me most was the contrast between what this school represented and what the University of Houston (which was literally minutes down the street) represented. The polished, progressive university campus represented intellect, advancement, culture, technology, exposure, and professionalism. Everything appeared to be organized and functioning at a high level, a vibrant city of its own that operated like a well-oiled machine.

On the other hand, the middle school I was assigned represented everything that was the polar opposite. Two miles down the road from the university campus, you were now in the inner city. Things looked totally different here—neglected, badly maintained, and clearly underserved. In addition to the area outside of the school being in clear disrepair, the inside of the school was even more deplorable.

To say that the kids' behavior was out of control would be an understatement. To add insult to injury, the academic aptitude was unfathomable, as many of the students did not know basic addition and subtraction skills. Just in case you don't have kids of your own, or can't remember when you learned simple math, allow me to refresh your memory. Students are introduced to basic addition and subtraction in the first grade and learn to add and subtract two-digit numbers in the second grade. The kids that I was working with were in *middle school*.

Everything about this school was chaotic and broken. It wasn't one of those situations where one might say, "Oh, it just looks a little out of sorts here. Once you pull back the layers, you'll see that everything is really under control." Nope. Nothing about this school was under control. Teachers' tires were being flattened. Kids regularly cursed out their teachers. Remember, I was a teenager (19 years old) at the time I was witnessing all of this. Even in my youthfulness, I knew that something was very wrong. I remember thinking, *There's no way that this can be what schools look like for students who look like me.* At that moment, I clearly understood why my mom woke me up at 5:30 AM to attend a school nearly halfway across the city for what she referred to as a "decent education."

After several weeks of working at my assigned middle school, the semester ended, and we went into the Christmas holiday. During my break, I had a lot of time to think, reflect, and process the experience I encountered during my stint with the middle schoolers. In January 1997, I returned to the University of Houston, switching my major from pharmacy to education. It was a no-brainer. I had already earned enough credit hours so that all I had to do was take the education courses required for an undergraduate degree in education. I graduated that next December. I considered the switch to be an all-around win-win: not only was I able to graduate a lot earlier than I would have if I'd continued pursuing my pharmacy degree, but I was able to embark on a career that would allow me to affect change in the impressionable lives of kids. Kids who looked like me but weren't afforded the same educational opportunities as me. I wanted to do something that would make a real, sustainable impact in the lives of others, and I knew education was the perfect context for this. I had seen with my own eyes that there was much to do. Now, armed with my teaching certification and a passion for serving young people, it was time to step out and do it.

The First Step: Middle School

When I graduated from the University of Houston, my first job was working as a seventh and eighth-grade history and English teacher for several years. This school and the community that surrounded it were a drastic change from the middle school where I tutored and the impoverished community in which it sat. This middle school was in a very affluent area of Houston. The majority of the students who attended were substantially well-off. They lived in elaborate 7,000 square feet, three-story homes, many of which had elevators in them, in the distinguished Galleria area. The neighborhood we served was synonymous with money. The parents were high-level professionals, such as doctors and lawyers. They had nannies, tutors, and any other support they needed to be successful. The stay-at-home moms drove brand new jaguars, and they made sure their children were dressed in the finest of clothing.

However, there was another dynamic at work that provided a significant learning opportunity for me. A select group of Hispanic students who lived in a set of apartments adjacent to the school also attended the school. Many of these students were English learners and were from working-class families. Each day, from first through sixth periods, I taught affluent kids who had tutors, academic support in the home, and who had never made a B in their lives. Then, for the rest of the school day, I had a group of kids who were challenged with language and learning and who did not have the same access to support resources that could ensure their academic success. The dichotomy between the two groups was glaring. It was interesting to be able to work in that type of environment and get to know both sets of kids as my first job, fresh out of school. Most importantly, I don't think it was an accident that I ended up in this context, one in which I was faced each day with confronting the realities of how access to resources and support impact how well students can do in academia.

The Second Step: Middle School, Again

During my tenure, my grandmother became ill, and I needed to find a position closer to home so that my mother and I were available to be home in a matter of minutes. Thankfully, not only was I blessed with something close, but it was an after school position where I could come in at a later time in the day. I was charged with preparing an array of activities for students to engage in at the end of the school day. Accepting this job was strategic. At the time, I wanted to see what it was like to concern myself with the well-being of students when there was no state assessment attached. How would my relationship change with students? What would I do when my only challenge was to engage kids in fun and exciting activities? Little did I know, it was all in God's will that this job would prepare me for the work to be done at the future schools. Making students feel special and valued while bequeathing them with fun, engaging activities was a huge part of my win at the school. This remains true today, more than 20 years after I first began working in leadership.

During this season, my grandmother became even more sickly, and I was charged with caring for her. Soon thereafter, she passed away. I was beyond devastated. To say the very least, she had been my ride or die. I helped plan her funeral and then quickly picked up the pieces, reclaiming my sense of normalcy, because she would not have accepted anything less. Her death marked the end of the after-school job and the beginning of something new.

After operating as the after-school coordinator for a couple of years, my principal pulled me aside and asked me to become the school improvement facilitator. This was a role in which I would basically operate in the same capacity as an assistant principal. However, the difference between the role of assistant principal and my role was that as the school improvement facilitator, my particular focus would be to assess every area of the school, determine how it could be improved, and put a plan into place to improve it. This marked the beginning of my interest in operating from a transformational perspective in my career. From that time on, I became intrigued by what it meant to look at a school and ask, "How can I make this campus better?" I gladly accepted the position and functioned as a school improvement facilitator. Both the opportunity and the myriad challenges that the position offered excited me, and I couldn't wait to begin!

The strategy for how to improve the middle school was left up to me; it was a completely self-guided approach. On my first day, I remember thinking, *Okay, I'm here now. What am I going to do?* The answer that came to mind: start with a needs assessment! I listed every single area of the school and made a list of questions to ask that would help me assess two things: the current condition of the school and how it could be improved. Armed with my list of assessment questions, I commenced with human capital. The staff and faculty of a school drive everything that happens, so it made sense to begin with them.

I began with assessing the school's human resources. I went around to every single teacher's classroom. I did frequent walkthroughs of the classes, conducting frequent assessments on the rapport that they had with their students, their knowledge of the content area they were teaching, how well they delivered the content knowledge to the students, and how students were performing on the assessments that the teachers gave them.

After gathering this data, I asked myself questions like:

- What type of teachers do we have?
- How qualified are the teachers?
- Are the teachers effective with their students?
- If I could replace anyone in this building, who would I replace?
- Why would I replace this individual, and with whom would I replace him/her?

Once I answered these questions, I recorded the results of my analysis. For example, some of the conclusions were:

- This person may be a good teacher, but he/she's not a good teacher *here*.

- This person may be a good assessment writer, but you have them teaching art. What is more needed on your campus?

- This person may be very much liked by the students, but he/she isn't producing anything in terms of advancing them academically.

After this, the final step was to take action. I had to strategically figure out how to negotiate with the teachers who weren't best for kids to not return the following year. We had some amicable separations, but for others, there were sad goodbyes. This would go on to become a standard practice that I engaged in on every campus that I would work on throughout my career. The very first thing that I assess is the teachers. I always begin with asking the question, "Who is best for kids and who is not?" If they're not best for kids, regardless of how long they've occupied the position, how well-liked they are, and how connected they are to the staff and students, they have to go. Transformational leaders have to be willing to make strategic staffing decisions in order to produce the best possible outcomes.

As difficult as it was to make these tough decisions, I had to remind myself, literally every single day, that this was about the kids. Nothing and no one else. You must ask yourself, "If my kid were in their class, would I be satisfied?" Every student is someone's child! I repeat: every student is someone's child, and they deserve the best. This was not about friendship, loyalty, or possibly being responsible for the teachers' livelihood (I know, I know, that sounds harsh, but I couldn't imagine my kids having a subpar education because administration was afraid of the ramifications of retiring someone that was ineffective). I fully understood that my decisions would be unpopular with some—those who were being asked to leave, their fellow teacher-friends they were leaving behind, some of the parents, and even many of the students. However, I entered into education with the specific goal of making a positive difference in the lives of children, and I knew without a shadow of a doubt that the decisions I was making were in their best interests. As long as kids' lives were being improved by the actions I took, I could live with being disliked or unpopular with the adults.

After assessing the faculty, I moved on to the campus safety. During this assessment phase, I asked questions such as:

- What does the safety look like on the campus?
- Where do people need to be placed in terms of monitoring?
- How are guests allowed in the building?
- What's the pick-up policy?
- How many fights happen on this campus?
- Why are the fights happening?
- Where and when do the fights happen?
- Who monitors the area where the fights tend to occur?
- Who's doing lunch duty?
- How many kids are in lunch at the same time?
- How is the food served to the kids?
- What's the quality of the food?
- How quickly do the students make it through the lines?
- How much time do they have to sit down to eat, and is this enough time?

Following this, I would always look at the systems and processes of the campus to ensure that they were streamlined. I accomplished this by asking questions like:

- What systems does the campus have in place?

- How efficiently does each of the systems run?

- What people are in place driving each system?

- Are the systems working, and how do we know?

- How long have these systems been in place?

- Are the processes that make this system work documented and shared with everyone?

- Are we considerate of working parents' time when we consider how long processes take?

- What systems need to be developed or refined to better serve students and parents?

I call these first three areas that I always begin with assessing as a transformational leader "The Big 3": safety, faculty, and systems. I should mention that these questions only represented about 10% of the questions that I asked when assessing the campus as the school improvement facilitator. There are *far* too many detailed questions and too many areas to mention in the pages of one book. However, these questions represent the gist of where I began when identifying what needed to be improved in the school. Once I answered these questions, I recorded the results of my analysis. With a team, I made adjustments to the school's policies, communicated these new policies to the administration, faculty, and students, oversaw the implementation, monitored the outcomes, and made further adjustments as necessary, based on the initial outcomes. Again, no one likes change, so adapting to the new policies that I set in place were not always done with a smile. However, my utmost concerns were the safety of the school, the academic progress of the students, and the development of a culture that made students want to come to school, rather than stay away from it.

After beginning with assessing these essential primary areas, I went on to assess every other area of the school, all the way down to the systems, processes, and people that undergirded them. These areas ran the gamut—instruction and academic aptitude, curriculum, student support, graduation rates, budget, teacher accountability, professional development, culture, student behavior and discipline, facility appearance—and a multitude of other areas that needed to be assessed. After assessing each area, I asked two fundamental questions: "Is this area operating on a functional level or not? If not, what can I do to make it better?" Then, I took the time to create an easy-to-follow, highly-detailed and organized plan.

By the time this process made it to the Houston-area high school where I served as principal, I had created what I call a "campus bible," which is a book that contains a plan for every area you can think of in the school. All you have to do is open it up to whatever section you want to know about, and you'll find a comprehensive plan that tells you exactly how the area is supposed to operate, along with detailed steps on what to do when executing a particular task in that area. For example, there's a plan for hiring. There's a plan for safety. There's a plan for how to disaggregate data. There's a plan for when the professional learning communities meet. There's a plan for every duty area. There's a plan for what should happen if a person is out for one or more days. There's a plan for everything in the campus bible.

When something was not working as it should have or I observed that something was not right, I would call a team meeting. Together, we would pull out the campus bible and open it to the proper area. I'd begin with, "Mr. Dotson, you're over safety. When I walked into the building this morning, so and so happened. That's not supposed to occur. Let's review what our plan says about what should be happening, and let's talk about why we're not following the plan." Then, we would discuss things from there. I'm an open-minded, team-oriented leader. If we were discussing how things were supposed to go based on the campus bible guidelines and determined that what was written was not the most effective or efficient approach, I was always open to discussions with my team about whether the plans needed to be altered. I was also very welcoming of their recommendations for how to change things that weren't working or needed modification. (Side note: I am not a micromanager. I must have people in my circle who I feel are able to do the work with minimal guidance, and I set them free to do so! I encourage trying new ideas, as long as it is not at the expense of student learning. But if I begin to notice that a member of my team needs excessive managing, they are not in the right position. Read that again!)

The most important thing, however, was for us to have a standardized approach for how we did everything in the school so that we were always on the same page. While I started this practice as the school improvement facilitator, I would go on to develop and operate by, and eventually perfect, the campus bible at every other campus that I would work at from that time forward.

After operating for one year as the school improvement facilitator, the principal of the school was asked by the superintendent to transfer to another campus. This new position was a high school that had been underperforming for quite some time. In fact, it was the first school in the state of Texas to ever be rated as "unacceptable" for so long that the state was ready to shut the doors for good. My principal, shocked by the offer, was ready for the challenge to turn the school around and do all she could to bring it up to an "acceptable" rating, allowing it to remain open. She asked me if I would join her. I said "Yes" before I considered any of the facts! I didn't question how much it paid, how high school would be different than middle school, or how far the school was from my home. I never questioned these things because at this point, she was the true transformational leader, and I'd follow her anywhere, knowing that if she asked me to go, it was a good move for both of us! I gladly accepted the challenge.

The Third Step: High School

I gave up my position as the school improvement facilitator to follow my principal at the time, J. Crump, to a failing high school. I began serving as the dean to approximately 2,000 students in June 2008.

As a part of the turnaround effort, our team was tasked with undertaking three significant actions: we replaced most of the administrative leaders on the campus, replaced many of the teachers, and separated the ninth graders, who were incoming freshmen, from the rest of the students. The ninth graders would be housed in their own building as a completely different campus, but on the same property: The Ninth Grade Center. Tenth, eleventh, and twelfth graders would remain housed in the main campus building. There was much work to do in undertaking this challenge, especially considering that we were working with two different campuses, and we had one year to get the work done. However, one of the recurring themes present throughout my career is that of courage in the face of adversity. I was ready to get started!

As the dean, my primary function was to build the academics. Because I began the position in June, there was much work to do over the summer. In fact, I was tasked with spearheading hiring about 120 teachers over the summer break in order to have a full staff in place for the upcoming school year. I spent the entire summer hiring, assisted by the school district's HR department, because they had to have the important salary discussions with the new staffers. The State had basically instructed us to replace approximately 75 to 80 percent of our staff, administration, and teachers, and that's exactly what we did. In total, the school had about 150 staff members, so roughly 120 of them had to be replaced.

After we assembled our new team of teachers and administrators, it was time to really roll up our sleeves and get started on the real work. We all knew that we were up against something extremely tough, because the school had been unacceptable for years. There was also an interesting dynamic at work because this was the first school in the district to ever be repurposed into two different campuses — a main campus and a ninth-grade campus. Because of this new, innovative approach, all eyes were on us. Now, we had the Texas Education Agency (TEA), the state agency that oversees public education in Texas, coming in regularly, monitoring what we were doing, watching us closely, and asking questions. Hard questions. However, their presence did not worry me (and they were actually extremely nice). I knew that we could get the job done, and because I was passionate about transformation, I knew that I was going to be an integral person in this charge.

The thing that gave me the greatest level of confidence about our ability to turn around this school on the verge of shut-down was that I felt really, really good about my hires. We had onboarded some great teachers over the summer. The one thing that I'd looked for during the hiring process was teachers who were highly knowledgeable in their content area. Because of this, I knew that even if we had to support the teachers, the one area that we would not have to support them in was the area of content. We might have had to support them in planning. We might have had to support them in classroom management. We might even have had to support them in student rapport. However, the one thing that we did not have to support them in was whether or not they knew the skill that they were charged with teaching to the students. For a school like this, that was critical. Everything was riding on their ability to bring the students' test grades up to par with acceptable state standards, and this had everything to do with the teachers' abilities to help students succeed in learning the content.

With our new, highly-qualified team in place, we worked incredibly hard that year. I'm certain that I was putting in 14 and 15-hour workdays every day. For most all of those hours, the teachers and administrators were working right along with me. I was coming in early and leaving out late. This didn't come without sacrifice. At that time, I had two small children, and I didn't live anywhere close to the school, so not only was I spending all of these hours at the school, but I also had a 3-hour commute – an hour and a half each way. It was a *truly* grueling time, but in the end, it was all worth it. By the end of the 2009 school year, we didn't just meet the state's standard expectations of going from unacceptable to acceptable; we exceeded them. (Side note: In hindsight, that type of commitment was damaging to my psyche as a mom. Here I was saving other people's children and feeling guilty that I was not seeing my own. This lesson taught me to work smarter and not harder and to never spend that much time away from my kids and family.)

We went from "Unacceptable" to "Recognized" in just one year! An outcome like this was unheard of and widely celebrated throughout the school district. For a school that had been unacceptable for so many years, the district just wanted to scratch the surface of being acceptable. Earning the designation of being recognized catapulted the school to a whole new category. That year, we received a visit from then Secretary of Education, Arne Duncan. Our work had been noticed! As I grew and learned, "transformational" was becoming more and more synonymous with who I was as a leader.

After this victory, the principal that was at the ninth-grade level received a promotion. He went on to become a school support officer working for the district, and this left a vacancy for the position. When I was tapped for the position, I was thrilled, but shocked.

Although what we accomplished was nothing short of amazing, I still only had one year of high school under my belt. Despite my doubts about myself, my principal didn't share these doubts, and just like the amazing leader she was, she pushed me to go! Thus, after one year operating as dean, I was asked to move from the main high school campus over to the ninth-grade school, serving as its leader.

The Fourth Step: Ninth Grade

In 2009, I became the leader of The Ninth Grade School, and I had to execute one focus: to get the ninth graders where they needed to be. Again, I knew that this was going to be a challenge, because ninth graders are a unique population. Education researchers have found that separating ninth graders from the higher grades in high school increases the odds of successful completion of high school for ninth graders. This is true for several reasons.

First, the transition to ninth grade can be as drastic of a change for students as the transition from elementary to middle school, so it is a critical period for them, almost like a mid-life crisis in their young lives. Additionally, ninth graders tend to be physically different than their older counterparts. To place a 14-year-old ninth grader next to a 20-year-old senior in class is literally to mix children with adults. They think differently, act differently, and have different needs. This was especially a consideration in high schools with large Hispanic populations, such as ours. Some might have come to the U.S. from Mexico, where they were classified as a tenth or eleventh grader, but once they were assessed by State of Texas standards, they were deemed a ninth grader. Therefore, a student could easily be a 19 to 20-year-old senior. There should be some type of separation between a child and an adult who is about to graduate and go on with life.

Then, the whole culture of high school is new for ninth graders; incoming freshmen don't know anything about credits, because they've never had them before. They have no clue about college entrance exams, getting prepared for college, and other brand new (and often intimidating) things that they are introduced to upon entering high school. Students are really needy at this level. Without close attention and support, they can potentially become so frustrated that they no longer want to go to school, resulting in them becoming a dropout. What can help them a great deal is knowing someone is looking for them (at school) every day and monitoring their grades. Incoming freshmen do not really understand that if they earn poor grades in the ninth grade, it could kill their GPA, and they'll need to spend the next three years trying to recover from their first year.

In consideration of the unique, specific needs of ninth graders, a lot of the research suggests that they need tailored help, specialized counseling, and assistance with making the transition into high school. By isolating the ninth graders into a smaller community of their own (because it's easy to get lost in the numbers in a larger high school population) with staff and teachers dedicated to addressing their specific needs, building a rapport with them, and developing close relationships with them, they have a better chance of successfully transitioning into high school and graduating.

As the new leader of the ninth-grade school, my biggest initiatives were to ensure that we had a 97 percent or better movement rate (from ninth to tenth grade). This could only happen if the students were passing their courses and their finals. If we could ensure that these things were happening, all together, they would average out to the students being ready to go from the ninth to the tenth grade. All of the education research, which I'd empowered myself with when I began the position, had indicated that if students didn't do well in the ninth grade, this was an indicator that there was a high probability that they would drop out of school. I was determined to ensure that we would not have a dropout problem under my watch as leader of the ninth-grade school.

I began the mission the same way I always had when approaching a new challenge: I created a team. One of the sub-teams was a district mandated DRIP team — Dropout Recovery and Intervention Plan. We would meet every Friday about any kid who had three or more absences. Once we ran reports to identify who the kids were, we would call them to find out why they'd missed school. We'd call them into the office and ask them directly, "What's going on? Why didn't you come to school?" If they weren't at school, we made home visits. We had personal relationships with the majority of our kids. I hate to tell you, but the more you discover as you peel back the layers, the harder you'll want to fix what ails the school, the community, and most of all, each student.

There were lots of reasons why our ninth graders were missing school. Some of them were pregnant. Some of them had kids they had to take care of at home. Some of them were taking care of ill parents. Some of them were taking care of younger sisters and brothers. Others simply saw no purpose for school. One young man who'd missed multiple days was called into my office. He had the number 44 tattooed in green ink in old English letters on his arm and on the top of his hand. I was sure that this tattoo had not been done in a tattoo parlor, and my hunch was correct. He told me it had been done while he was in a juvenile detention center. "What does it mean?" I asked. He burst into laughter! "Ms.! You don't know what that means?" Ashamedly, I was upset about not being as familiar as I should have, but it did not stop me from asking again. It turned out that not only did I not know what it meant, but I was saying it wrong. He proudly referred to it as "The Fo-Fo," not "Forty-Four" as I was saying it. The numbers represented the bus line number for that area, which was known as Acres Homes.

After our exchange of laughter (and my speech about tattooing a bus line on your skin), I would look for him every day and refer to him by my nickname for him, "Four-Four." Knowing that I was looking for him daily improved his attendance tremendously. Did he have multiple issues? Of course, he did. All the more reason to give him the extra push!

Just as I made it a purpose to look for him every day, everyone on that campus had the same caring, intentional mindset. We understood that our role was to get kids in school, and keep them in school, regardless of why they had been missing. We made it a point and our mission to listen carefully. What we could fix, we fixed. For example, if we could connect them with a local daycare to watch their kids or their siblings, that's what we did. If they were sick and needed medical attention and we could get them to doctor's appointments in the afternoon so that they didn't have to miss school, we did it. If we could talk to their mom about the fact that these ninth graders were not the parents of their six- or seven-year-old brothers and sisters, and how they as parents needed to drop the smaller siblings off at school so that their ninth graders weren't late every single day, then that's what we did. We provided a lot of emotional support and problem solving, advocating for the students and helping them address things that they could not address for themselves.

We were also fortunate to have the nonprofit organization "Communities in Schools" (CIS) on our campus. This is a national organization that works with public schools, building relationships and providing services that empower students who are at-risk to stay in school, excel academically, and succeed in life. They stepped in to help us address some of the things that we just could not fix for our students. For example, we were able to send kids to CIS when they needed free counseling services. CIS was able to direct the students to places where they could receive those services and support, free of charge, so that they could be better prepared to come back to school. CIS and the support they provided, along with access to resources they offered, played a critical role in helping us do our job in serving the students in the ninth-grade school.

In addition to servicing the social needs of our students that were affecting their ability to come to school, of course, we made sure that we also focused on their academic needs. We extended the school day for our students: they came in early and stayed late in the day. We provided tutorials for students who needed additional academic assistance, both early morning and late afternoon. We added in additional classes for our students so that they had cushion and wiggle room; just in case they performed poorly in one class, the credits that they earned from extra, additional classes could make up for it. The addition of these extra classes ensured that the students had the opportunity to earn all of the credits they needed to go on to the tenth grade. The former principal hired quite a few young, eager teachers the year prior, and they were eager to help us accomplish our goals with the students. These teachers were always available, so that really helped a lot in getting the students where they needed to be in preparation for the tenth grade.

We also ensured that students were acclimated to the new expectations of high school concerning rules, discipline, and organization. This was perhaps our biggest challenge of all, especially because we were undertaking it on a traditionally underserved campus with students who were accustomed to doing what they wanted. Many of them operated out of a, "Who's going to check me?" mentality, and we had to teach them that in high school, we will all check you. I had to come in as a principal and say, "No, we are not going to skip any classes. No, we are not going to fight in the cafeteria. No, we are not going to disrespect our teachers." When they saw me on my way towards them, they would say, "Here you come with all the rules, Lady!" I grew accustomed to being "that lady," the one they thought was coming to kill their fun. However, I knew that with each bit of coaching and correction, I was preparing them for something greater, so I persisted. I was willing to be the unpopular one as long as it was going to help them grow and benefit them in the future. Transformational leaders always remain focused on the big picture – accomplishing the mission – even in the midst of eye rolls, groaning, and complaining! Soon, that all ended, and they became my children for life. The secret formula: remain fair and consistent.

At the end of that school year, 97 percent of our kids successfully matriculated from ninth to tenth grade. We were very proud of our work that year, and the district was proud of us, too. Again, my brand as a transformational leader in the school district was strengthened as a result of the outcomes that I was able to lead a team to produce at the Ninth Grade School. Once again, we were not just acceptable; we were a recognized campus! This would serve as another successfully executed training exercise in developing my skills as a transformational leader, preparing me for even greater challenges ahead.

The Fifth Step: Back to Middle School I Go!

In 2012, I was asked to take on another turnaround campus challenge. I became the principal at a small inner-city school that was a change from the ninth-grade school at which I'd formerly served. I went from leading a majority-Hispanic ninth-grade school to leading a predominantly-Black sixth through eighth-grade middle school. Although I say majority, the numbers for the Hispanic population were rapidly increasing. Because of that, I asked my AP from the ninth-grade academy to join me. He was a bilingual, no-nonsense leader – exactly what I knew I needed. This was a school that had dealt with being underserved for years and I knew that everyone needed to feel heard and serviced. The school was populated with underprivileged kids, but these kids were at a different level. The nickname for the community in which they lived was "the Dead End." It got its name because, years before I became the principal, the school actually sat on Martin Luther King Boulevard, which was a dead-end street at the time. Although the street had been opened up years prior to my becoming the principal of the school, the area still retained its nickname; it connoted the Dead End fate that the residents of the community would ultimately face, simply by virtue of being born there.

This was an area that was disadvantaged, underserved, and forgotten. Anyone who doubted the truth of this needed only to look around at the living conditions of those in the community. The apartment complex that was next door to the school was so broken down that some of our campus leaders wrote to our district representative and the City of Houston about it, leading the City to finally declare it unlivable. Many of our kids were living without air, which is extremely concerning in a city like Houston, where the temperature can often exceed 100 degrees in the summertime. Lots of our kids had also grown accustomed to not having heat in the wintertime. Even worse, there were times when a number of our students lived without running water. One can easily research news articles written about the area after it was discovered that people in the area sometimes had to go out and dig their own ditches to get a water line to work. It was unreal.

In the "Dead End" community that surrounded the middle school, the history, conditions, and culture of the community seemed to affirm to its residents that this was it; there was nothing greater that one could attain outside of this neighborhood. There was no better future to be had. The "Dead End" was an area that was so filled with violent, criminal activity that was so dangerous, that even the police were reluctant to drive through it. I describe this community in such detail so that you understand that students who lived in the area faced a great deal of barriers.

A week before the students were to return to the middle school, I had already started on my mission to clean up the school. I was meeting with district lawyers regarding a teacher that had been illegally using campus fundraising money. As I drove out of the parking garage, my cell phone rang, but I missed the call. I usually never return calls from unidentified numbers, but something in my spirit told me to do so. It was a police officer telling me that my father had been involved in a major car accident. By the time I reached the hospital, I was lost and confused. Thankfully, my husband worked at the hospital and met me at the door. We inquired about my father and were told that they had no patient by his name. When en route, I had called my family, which had made me significantly more panicky, and I thought that I had missed the officer telling me the correct hospital. I hurriedly called the officer back, and he assured me that I was indeed at the correct hospital. However, because my father had been life-flighted to the hospital, he had arrived under an alias. I swore to the officer that he'd never told me that, but he assured me he did.

I was a wreck; I was having a complete and total meltdown. My father was and always had been my rock. I got myself together as much as possible and walked back in to meet my husband. Soon thereafter, my family arrived. We sat in the waiting room sharing fond memories. After a few hours of working on my father, the doctor walked in, kneeled next to me and my husband in the shadows with my family close, and announced that my father didn't make it. To say that I was devastated was an understatement. I stayed home a couple of days to make arrangements and grieve. However, on Monday morning, I returned to campus, ready for the challenge that lay ahead. It's exactly what my father would have told me to do.

When I accepted the challenge to turn around the campus, it was right around the time that the state accountability system changed. The Texas Assessment of Knowledge and Skills (TAKS) standardized test was being replaced with a new test: the State of Texas Assessments of Academic Readiness (STAAR) test was taking its place. The STAAR test was more difficult than the TAKS test. While a student can pass the TAKS test by learning things through rote memorization, the STAAR test required students to think at a higher level. This meant that not only was I coming in to turn around an underperforming campus, but I was doing it at a time when attaining success was being made more challenging.

Because of the switch to the more-demanding STAAR test, the first year that the assessment was offered didn't count for any of the schools. It was like a "learning year" in terms of standardized testing, allowing the schools extra time to prepare the students. However, even though the scores didn't count in terms of accountability for the state, the first-year test scores would at least allow us to see where our students stood so we would know how much work was ahead of us, to prepare them for when the scores would count for accountability.

The year began, and, together, my team and I created what we thought was an amazing week worth of professional development. Excited about embarking upon the work, another devastating call came in. A student that was very popular at school had had an accident while riding on the hood of a car and passed away. Thus, my first week of the new school year had been plagued with two deaths. That wasn't all. Teachers stood up in faculty meetings and proclaimed, "These kids," as if they belonged to no one, "can't learn like other kids!" It was clear that we had a major teacher issue. We were rolling the dice from there on out. Even after you engage in planning and put in the hard work, if you have teachers who don't believe in kids, there's no certainty that you'll win. From the moment I heard these comments, it was a big red flag; I knew that we did not have the right teachers in place. We needed to get the right teachers in place in order to make things work at the school.

As if all of this was not enough, we dealt with excessive mice and snakes (both literally and figuratively) in the building! One day, I received a call to come to a classroom for an "emergency." I ran to the classroom. Pacing myself so as not to appear alarmed, I entered the room to be met by a room full of calm students' eyes when I walked in the door. I was perplexed; I had been called to the classroom for an "emergency," and yet everyone looked surprisingly unbothered. *If this is an emergency, why does everyone look so calm?* I wondered. I locked eyes with the teacher. "How may I help you? Is everything okay?" I asked calmly. He simply pointed down next to his desk. I eased over and looked down toward where he was pointing. On the floor were four rats stuck to a sticky pad and squealing loudly. Before that day, I had never, in my entire life, known that rats squealed. What I did know was that I was more afraid of rats than any other animal in this world! However, I had a classroom full of middle school kids watching me. With great composure, I asked each of them to stand up and I filed them out of the classroom, one by one. When the room was emptied, the plant operator came in and removed the singing rats. I immediately had the school fumigated – a move that I think made the snakes appear. The pest issue was compounded by other issues that were happening simultaneously. There was a condemned building nearby that was being torn down, which inevitably affected our school. There were also teachers headed out on family and medical leave left and right, leaving us short of teaching staff without consideration of the kids' needs. There was a lot going on all at once! Despite it all, I knew that I could not allow the school to be plagued. Kids deserved to come to a clean environment free of roaches, rats, snakes, and most importantly, teachers who don't care. We were on a mission, and nothing was going to stop us!

The first year STAAR test results weren't really a surprise to us. After all, I came to the school to take on a campus turnaround project, so I already knew the students were behind. The STAAR results would just help me to pinpoint how behind our students were. As expected, our kids did very poorly on the test, with the results indicating that they were three to five grade levels below where they needed to be. In fact, the scores showed us that we had a significant two-fold challenge on our hands: we needed to teach our kids to start thinking more deeply, and at the same time, we needed to teach them the basic skills that they didn't receive at the elementary school level, bringing their academic proficiencies up to par. We had a big task ahead of us, but I was sure that with the right team and with a lot of long days and hard work, we could get it done. I knew that this was a smart campus; if we put the right people in the right places, we could get the school, the students, and the STAAR results where they needed to be by the time the next STAAR assessment was offered.

Speaking of the right team, we faced some considerable challenges in that area. First, there was a lot of turnover of teachers and staff in my first year after we took the first STAAR test. This was primarily because they didn't know whether the campus was going to be labeled "Improvement Required." They didn't want to take any chances in sticking with the school and suddenly being left without a place to work because of its failing standards. The STAAR results showed just how far behind the students were, and a lot of teachers thought that there was no way they could be brought up to grade level by the following year. Then, not only were the STAAR scores very low, but the student attendance was also low. It seemed inevitable that massive changes had to be made.

Undaunted, I approached the transformational challenge in the same way I always had: with the staffing. I knew that hiring the right teachers was going to be a big part of turning the school around. I set out to get people in there who would be dedicated to do the extensive work, who knew what these kids needed, and who were willing to offer it to them. Most importantly, I hired teachers who didn't need help with the actual content they were responsible for teaching; they had to be very knowledgeable about their subject area.

Next, after the team was in place, we began analyzing the STAAR data, disaggregating it so that we could better understand where our students were falling short. We trained the teachers on how to read, interpret, and draw conclusions based on their analysis. Most of them had never had to work with data in this way before. We spent *a lot* of time disaggregating and analyzing the data because what we interpreted from it would be used to guide the direction of the work we would do with the students.

After we established the direction of the instruction that we need- ed to focus on with the students, we then examined what it would look like to roll the lessons out to a student. In these exercises, we specifically looked at *how* teachers were teaching what they were teaching, and whether or not they were effective in how they taught it. We would ask, "What does it look like to teach this par- ticular content effectively so that students really get it?" Then, we did what I called "at bats." These were sessions in which we met in our professional learning communities and practiced teaching a lesson amongst other adults. The teachers literally had to teach the lesson they planned to teach the kids to the team and me, the exact way they were going to teach it to the kids, and we would provide them with feedback. If there was anything that we, the adults, didn't understand, we let the teacher know. Then, the teach- er would tweak the lesson, or the delivery, based on our feedback. This way, when teachers got in front of kids, the lesson was some- thing that the kids would clearly understand. It would ensure that after the teacher taught her heart out, she wouldn't be looking at a sea of blank faces in the classroom. This planning and preparation process was detailed, tedious, and time consuming, but it was what was necessary to see our kids succeed, and we were dedicated to doing whatever we needed to do to help them win.

Winning didn't come easily in the Dead End. Our students were challenged in their home lives in *every* way that kids could possibly be challenged – food, clothes, no air conditioning in the summer, no heat in the winter, inconsistent access to running water, being surrounded by violent crime and drugs, and living in poverty-stricken conditions. Added to this, they had to overcome challenges at school, such as playing catch up to learn all the things they missed in elementary school, while simultaneously learning what they were responsible for knowing in their current grade in middle school. The odds were stacked against them—and us—because there was so much work to do.

After we took the trial STAAR test the first year, the next three years following, we rated acceptable; our kids kept scarcely meeting the criteria. Each year, we would assess what we were doing and what we could be doing better to catch our students up. In year four, we failed. We were rated "IR" or "Improvement Required." This was definitely a blow to the gut. My first failure. My team was equally devastated. We vowed to come back the following year stronger than ever.

Over the summer, we were able to disaggregate the data to pinpoint what went wrong. We discovered that we had a really weak reading teacher, and because our campus was so small, one teacher could really have a significant impact on our students' results. We replaced the reading teacher, tightened our PLC's, analyzed the data again, and put systems in place that would hone in on the needs of each individual student. We implemented computer programs, tutors, and additional teachers. I fought like crazy to make these things happen for our kids! Then, finally, in the fifth year, our hard work paid off, and then some. We didn't just make standard, but we made standard plus earned *five* out of seven possible distinctions awarded by the Texas Education Agency! Distinctions are indicative of how much a school has increased in various subject areas and how much students have improved across the board, relative to other schools that look like us demographically. Such recognition is like getting a gold star from the State of Texas, and we received five of them! Success was sweet after four years of work! In the end, this campus, which was written off by many, had risen like a phoenix from the ashes. The reason: I was able to lead a hard-working team of self-sacrificing teachers and staff and turn it around when others thought doing so to be farfetched. This win further strengthened my brand as a transformational leader who had the ability to lead change against all odds—and this was unquestionably an against all odds type of year! This was a year a female student was kidnapped, and we took chase on foot (and by car) after the culprit; a student stole a teacher's wallet, and after police were called, guns were drawn; over $100,000 worth of laptops were stolen and sold at the neighborhood pawn shop (and within the apartment complex across the street from the school); a high-speed chase culminated in our parking lot, knocking over our gate; and a large snake was found slithering around campus — and it was not in or from our science lab! This. Was. A. Year. But we WON, and we WON BIG!

The Sixth Step: District Level Supervisor

With another victory under my belt following the transformation at the middle school level, I was exhausted and ready for something different. Charles Foust, my mentor and supervisor at the time, stressed the importance of not worrying about the outside noise – dig in and get it done – don't fail. "Once you are known as a turnaround principal you can write your ticket anywhere!" and he was right! With his recommendation, I was recruited by my district to take on a new position. The new role, which was a promotion, was being a school support officer (SSO), serving 16 different schools in the district. In this position, I essentially did what the title of the position suggested: provided support. I supported principals when they had parent issues, teacher issues, and resource issues. When providing solutions, I always did so from a transformational leadership style, advising the principals on how to remedy their issues in a way that was motivating and inspiring, helping them to coach, mentor, and develop their teachers and staff towards success, modeling the attitude, culture, and behaviors they wanted to see in their followers, and helping them to plan and organize for success.

Ultimately, I ensured that the principals had everything they needed to run their schools, did walkthroughs with them to identify any areas of need or improvement, helped them to evaluate their teachers to determine whether or not they were on par, and led them in identifying next steps and solutions if things were not as they should be in the school. My own experiences as a transformational leader made me a key asset in this position. It was this job that I was happily functioning in when I was approached with an opportunity to take on the greatest transformational challenge of my career: a well-known and beloved but failing Houston-area high school.

The Seventh Step: A Failing Houston-area High School

In December 2016, there were some rumblings that there were 10 schools that were going to be closed down by the Texas Education Agency the following year if they did not meet their STAAR assessment expectations. At the time this news began circulating throughout the educational community, it had nothing to do with me. There were 283 schools in the district, and as a school support officer, I was only responsible for 16 of them. Further, none of my schools were a part of the 10 that had been threatened with closure because of an unacceptable status.

That same month, my supervisor called me and informed me that a well-known and historical Houston-area high school needed additional support. It happened to be one of the 10 that was slated to be closed down if they didn't get out of unacceptable status that year. I was like, "Okay, cool. I'm in." I didn't mind helping at all. They added this school to the list of schools that I supported. This was a unique support assignment, unlike any other. Every school was assigned one school support officer. However, because this particular school was in such bad shape, they didn't just have one school support officer assigned to the school. They had a school support officer assigned to *every subject area*! That was five SSOs working with this one school, something totally unheard of in our district.

My supervisor put me in charge of providing support to the biology department. Keep in mind, biology was neither my background nor my specialty, and to add icing to the cake, I was pregnant (and my brain worked at 90% during these times)! In any case, I was willing to fill in wherever needed and provide the support that was necessary. It was my job. It couldn't be too bad, I thought. I was only slated to be there two or three days out of the week to supervise biology, so it wasn't an unreasonable ask, especially given the fact I still serviced my other campuses.

Once I started going to the high school throughout the week to supervise the biology department, I was pleased to see some of my students who had attended the middle school that I was previously principal of. Although the campuses were just down the street from each other, the students that I'd served there weren't zoned to go to this high school. Some of them had just moved closer to the school, or simply chose to attend this particular high school instead of the high school that they were zoned to attend. I mention this because seeing my former students in this high school environment helped me understand something important about the school. The school had earned a reputation for being filled with "bad" kids. However, these were *my* kids, and I knew them *well*. I knew for a fact that they weren't "bad" kids. They might not have been on their best behavior at the high school, but it wasn't because they were "bad." It was that the adults who were responsible for directing them simply allowed them to do unacceptable things. Just like any other kids, they were going to push the limits and do whatever they were allowed to do. The "bad" label simply didn't apply!

As one of the subject area SSOs for the high school, I went in and provided support and assistance to the biology department. I didn't do anything out of the ordinary in regard to how I typically approach a turnaround challenge. I engaged those in the department using a transformational approach. I focused on improving the staffing, trained the teachers on how to collect, disaggregate, read and analyze data, helped them put together a plan for how to better instruct the students based on the results of the data analysis, and helped to create some systems, organization, and accountability for the department.

For example, when I first arrived in the biology department, the students had taken about seven tests. Based on the test score data, I asked the teachers to tell me the following: which students were going to pass the class, which students were in danger of failing the class, and who needed to go to tutorials? Then, I asked them to give me a prescriptive plan for each kid. Every one of the teachers was looking at me like I was speaking a foreign language. They had absolutely no idea what I meant. I realized I was going to have to start from square one. I said, "Okay. Where is your data?

What do you have?" They explained that the data was housed in the administration's offices. I asked, "Well, does he/she teach your class?" There was a collective "No." My next question seemed like an elementary one to me. I asked, "Then why would he/she have the data and not you?"

We proceeded to dig around until we found a little USB flash drive that contained all the data they needed on their students. I went into their professional learning community (PLC) with them and projected the data on the screen. I took them step by step through how to read and interpret the data, and I led them in exercises that helped them to draw conclusions about the direction they should go with their instruction, based on the data. On that first day, we looked at the data to determine how many kids would pass the biology portion of the STAAR test if they had to take it that day. Out of the 170 kids for which we had data, only 13 kids would have actually passed the test, if the test was given that particular day. From there, we asked the critical questions: What are we teaching? How are we teaching it? Are we teaching it the same way that the test is testing it? And if not, what do we need to change? Working with the teacher development specialist, we put a plan into place. Then, we executed the plan, putting in a ton of extra hours, energy, and dedication in order to help the kids win.

To make a long story short, at the end of the school year, when the standardized test scores came back in May, biology was the only department in the entire school that had made substantial gains. However, while the department I supported made gains, the school had not made it out of the Improvement Required (IR) status.

The district realized in April of 2017 that it was time to take drastic action. They set out to change the leadership of the school for the next school year. I was asked to take on the biggest turnaround challenge of my career: becoming the principal of this beloved Houston-area high school.

Chapter 2
Transformational Leadership Tips

TLT 2.1
Build Your Brand

- Decide what your educational focus will be and become impeccably good at it!

TLT 2.2
Be Willing to Make Tough Decisions

- Make decisions not based on who you like or dislike but on what a person or program significantly offers children.

TLT 2.3
Create Systems That Work

- With so many urgent issues and challenges vying for your attention, resist taking a random approach to problem solving and turning things around. Instead, develop systems for dealing with issues and for taking a planned, strategic approach to change. Most of all, ensure that everyone on the team knows and is held accountable for operating according to the systems you put in place.

TLT 2.4
Never be Afraid to Take on the Challenge

- View the end game. Ask yourself, "What will this look like when I am done?"

> "
>
> Nearly all of [the school's] students deal with the effects of deep, intractable poverty that create longer odds for success in school. [This campus] is surrounded by census tracts where the median household income is about $20,000, among the lowest in Texas. Sunnyside often has been labeled the most dangerous neighborhood in Houston. Few large urban public school systems have succeeded with students from such disadvantaged backgrounds.
>
> - Jacob Carpenter, *Houston Chronicle*, Sunday, July 15, 2018
>
> "

3

The First Year at the School

Accepting the Challenge to Bring Order to a Chaotic Campus in Two Months

llow me to set the scene. I was 40 and pregnant with my third child when I was asked to become principal of a high school in an area that the FBI had tagged as one of the most dangerous zip codes in the entire United States. Only two words came to mind when I thought of this high school: JE - SUS! There were three or four fights on the campus every day, and during some of those fights, there may have been a bag of rocks found on a student, concealed in a cotton drawstring bag, used as a weapon to defend oneself. Even worse, this was the kind of neighborhood where if there was a fight on campus, a mob of 20 or more people from all over the neighborhood would come – parents, cousins, friends; you name it. To heighten the situation, they had full-out brawls that literally shut down the street in front of the school. Of course, this was not technically the school's jurisdiction, but when they were the students that you were responsible for, you saw it through. When the kids weren't spectators watching a fight, it seemed as if they spent more time hanging out in the hallways and restrooms than they spent in class. There were rumors of kids smoking marijuana and rolling dice in the restroom. Many of the kids, 50 or 60 each day, would defy the rules, leave campus for lunch, and ditch class for the remainder of the day. Little or no action was taken on this behavior. It appeared as if absolutely no influence (or authority) was able to make the kids comply with campus rules and expectations. I equated it to a scene from "Lean on Me."

This wasn't like the kind of school that had just been forsaken in terms of academics; this school had been forsaken in terms of safety, culture, and civility as well. If you googled the campus, the first story that popped up was that of a murder that happened in the back field during a non-school sanctioned powder puff football game a few years before. Many students whose home school was zoned to be this failing high school, brilliant, ambitious kids who lived in the neighborhood, transferred away from the high school. They opted to attend schools outside of the neighborhood. Why? Because they knew that they would receive an "uninterrupted" education without having to deal with the perceived danger and risk that their local community high school had to offer. Think about it: they were petrified to go to the high school closest to their homes, even though the school was reflective of the neighborhood in which they lived.

My Initial Response to the Opportunity: Saying "*No!*" because of What I *Knew*

When my superiors approached me with the opportunity to become the principal of the high school, they essentially said, "We know your track record as a leader who can turn around campuses, and well, you've been working with the biology department as an

SSO, so you already know the students here. Would you be willing to take on this school as the principal?"

"Uhhh… no!" I answered. It was a reflex response. I didn't even think twice.

"Why not?" they asked.

My reply was simply, "Because I *know*."

What did I know about this high school that made my answer instantaneously "No?" A lot! The first thing I knew was something that my supervisors didn't know: I was five months pregnant. I wasn't 27 or 30 and pregnant, like I had been with my first two kids. I was 40. Another thing I knew was that this school was in an impoverished neighborhood. This was a disadvantaged school, and according to statistics, dangerous. Extremely dangerous. If you were to google its zip code, you would actually see that the Federal Bureau of Investigation considered it to be one of the most dangerous zip codes in the United States. Not one of the most dangerous in Houston. Not one of the most dangerous in Texas. One of the most dangerous in the *United States*.

Here's another thing that I knew about the high school: since the STAAR test had been implemented, the school had never met STAAR benchmarks. Not once. I had first-hand knowledge of the teacher situation from working there as an SSO. There were frequent teacher absences, data was not used to drive intentional instruction, and there was no clear plan for teaching. Teachers were guessing about what to teach, lacking command of their classrooms, all while kids were getting further and further behind. On an initial walkthrough of the classrooms, I saw many students who sat through their classes, disengaged, sometimes asleep, other times on their phone, not learning anything. Finally, one of the biggest things that I knew (but that no one dared mention, even though it was the elephant in the room) was that this was a political move. A big one. I had built a strong brand, a winning reputation, for being able to lead turnarounds in education, but this school was on a desolate island all by itself. My name was on the line. If the high school failed under my leadership, it would not only be the school that failed, but my name would be attached to that failure.

In light of all these factors, you can understand why I didn't jump at the opportunity to take the position. There were safety issues, student behavioral issues, big-time staffing issues, political issues, and there would be a *ton* of work to do to help the school recover from nearly a decade of failures to bring it up to par. On top of it all, I couldn't "jump" at the opportunity if I wanted to, because I was four months away from giving birth to my third child in what was considered a "geriatric" pregnancy. Nevertheless, after my initial reflex response declining the opportunity, I told them that I would think about it. There was a lot to digest as I considered whether or not this was the right career move for me to make.

Reconsidering the Opportunity: Thinking Beyond Myself to Create a Better Life for Others

People often asked me if I was ever afraid of going into a high school campus with this type of reputation. They asked this not only because I was about to have a baby, but because of the physical demands, long hours, inevitable exhaustion, and all that would be required for the job. Was I physically and mentally prepared? I was never afraid of the environment — neither the neighborhood nor the kids – and I never feared for my safety. To tell you the truth, I think I'm just too crazy to be afraid when I should be! The thing that intimidated me more than the danger of the neighborhood and school environment was how my family might be impacted if I accepted the job. I thought about what life was going to be like to have three kids and a demanding job, with an hour round trip commute each day. I wondered if taking on the role as principal of the high school might pull me away from my loved ones too much. That was a scarier thought than experiencing any physical harm in an unsafe environment.

During the time I took to contemplate whether or not I could make this job work, providing the students and the community with what they needed, I continued to worry whether or not I would have enough time for my children. How much time from my family would this job take? My oldest child was in high school. Would I miss any of his games because I had to be at my own high school's games? Would my own children feel neglected in any way because their mother would be working so much, even on the weekends? Would I be leaving my husband in a situation where he was overwhelmed with having to take care of everything during all of those hours I wasn't there? On top of it all, would I be neglecting my unborn child? Those were the thoughts that ran rampant through my mind and kept me up at night.

For a few days, about an hour or so each day, I went to a quiet place in my head. I felt like I could handle this; the safety issues, turning the school around, the students, etc. were never a concern for me. I had to remember that I had been well prepared to take on such challenges throughout my career. Succeeding as a transformational leader, even against the biggest obstacles and in the most hopeless situations, had become what gave me breath. I was especially prepared to take on the challenges that the high school presented that differed from working as a principal at the middle school; as discussed, the middle school was in a similar environment, exactly 3.5 miles down the road. I was becoming more and more confident that I could take on the challenge. Yet, there were questions that continued to linger in my mind. Did I *really* have the capacity to take on the challenge? Did I want it so badly that I'd be willing to, at times, forsake my family and personal life? I grappled with these questions to no avail, knowing that if I accepted the position, not only would my life change, but my family members' lives would be affected as well.

After much thought, countless conversations with my family, and lots of prayer and talking to God, I accepted the job, ready to take on the challenge. With my husband, kids, and family's full support, I was in a good place with my decision. Little did my Mom know, she would soon be moving in with us into our new home we were building—becoming the fabric that held our family in place. There's nothing like knowing you have a good, solid support system at home when you're about to embark upon something so immense. However, this was not what made the biggest difference in my decision to take on the challenge of turning around a school that had been failing for nearly a decade. What changed my mind was something bigger. Deeper… More significant and purposeful. The entity that made the biggest difference was an opportunity to change and transform lives. If you think back to my "why," or the reason that I entered into education as a career choice in the first place, you'll remember that this has been my motivation from the very beginning. The influence, titles, and building a name are great; however, the opportunity to change the trajectory of children's lives forever simply by transforming their educational experience? Well, that's priceless. How could I pass up an opportunity like this?

See, I know my own kids come from a good foundation where they don't have to worry about where a meal will come from, where they will sleep for the night, or if there will be hot running water for them to shower. I also know that my children will be educationally sound, being afforded the opportunity to engage in multiple opportunities that will push their thinking and intellect in a healthy environment. I have the knowledge and ability to send them to the best schools, for them to explore places I could only dream of at their age, and for us to go on family vacations where we partake in new adventures and experiences. I know that my children are going to be cultured (well, the oldest two are boys so let's just say they'll say, "Excuse Me!" from time to time) and well-exposed; they attend what I like to call "local cultural experiences" by going to places such as the Houston Symphony, the Houston Ballet and the Houston Opera, to name a few. Whether they enjoy it or not is another story, but I introduce them to these types of experiences because I understand the value of exposure. I've worked really hard to get to the point in life where I can offer an upbringing like this to my kids so that they can have the best possible chance of succeeding on their own terms in life. As a result, my kids are growing up believing that the sky is the limit, even as young African American men amid the events that played out in the summer 0f 2020. They sincerely believe that they can be whatever they want to be, do whatever they want to do, go as far in life as they want to go, be as big and powerful as they are destined to be by working hard, and they are well-prepared, educated, and equipped with the skills that they need to make it happen. They have a broad, expansive worldview. They know that the only limits on their lives are the ones they place on themselves.

However, what kind of world will my kids live in as adults if the majority of the population doesn't have these experiences? Who would they be surrounded by if those individuals didn't have access to a good education, support, and exposure? Nothing happens in a vacuum. When our society produces children who are undereducated and underprepared to succeed in life, everyone is affected in some way. The community that surrounded this high school was a prime example: we were looking at a whole community that had been affected by this one school, simply because the kids did not have the advantages, or access, to the knowledge and resources to make things happen or the luxury to be exposed. How lucky would a group of individuals be, called upon to be educators, if they were deemed with the responsibility to provide these kids with the education, exposure, and experiences they deserved, so that they, too, just like my kids (and I'm sure yours), would have the opportunity to be anything they wanted to be in life versus being pigeon-holed into lower-level employment and poverty?

Ultimately, the bottom line was that kids were suffering. Although it could have been a bad political move for me to take the position, I believed it to be an even worse decision to not accept it. As a mother and educator, I could not sit by and watch kids do poorly and not be given a fighting chance in life, simply because adults didn't care. It wasn't that the kids didn't know what to do, how to do it or have a desire to be better. It was that some of the adults, for whatever reason, weren't giving these young adults their best. I knew that the problem with this high school was not a kid issue. Even though the students at the school had developed a reputation of misbehaviors, being unmotivated, and unmanageable, this school's issue was an adult issue. Yes, I said it - It was a planning issue. It was a care issue. It was a heart issue. It was a work ethic issue. These are all adult issues. The students were doing what they were doing because the adults were not doing what they should have been doing.

I onboarded as the principal of the high school in April 2017, with about eight weeks of school remaining for the year. A few months later, in August 2017, an unfortunate natural disaster crippled the city of Houston right around the time school was slated to begin. Hurricane Harvey produced catastrophic rainfall and flooding, which led to many Houston schools being closed for an extended amount of time. It decimated the city. Soon after (a day or so) the storm passed, I gave birth to a beautiful and healthy baby! This unfortunate event had a silver lining for me, and that was KayLani Rose. Because of the storm, the school opening was pushed back 10 days, so although I had an unexpected c-section, and was slated to be out at least eight weeks, I was able to manage only missing about four weeks of actual school and returned five weeks after giving birth.

We assumed that missing those 10 days of school would somehow make the commissioner have pity on us and say that our account-ability would be waived, but that did not happen (at least not for our school). Our school remained one of 10 schools in the district that had to meet standards in order to avoid being shut down. However, in April 2018, six of those schools got a reprieve because of how much they were affected by Hurricane Harvey; they were given an additional year to meet standards. Four schools did not get a reprieve, and ours was one of them. We still had to meet stan-dards by June of 2018, or our campus, the only high school of the four schools on the list, would be closed. That was a lot of pressure, and a lot riding on our high school's turnaround.

Although our high school had earned a less-than-stellar reputa-tion in the Houston community, people still loved it – greatly. It was a legendary Houston institution. No one, and I mean *no one*, wanted the school to be closed down! Many of the city's politicians got involved in trying to do all they could to keep the school open. The local media published articles about the potential closing of the school, and how it would disappoint many in the community for such a historical school to close its doors. Many Houstonians and Alum (both inside and beyond our school community) want-ed – and in some ways demanded – that it remain open. However, the bottom line was the bottom line: if the staff and student body didn't do the work and make the scores, the fate of the school was closure. Or at best, closed and opened as another school with all new faculty. I felt the weight of these sentiments on my shoulders every single day as the school's principal.

Getting Started: The First Year Observation Phase

Let me take you back a bit. I was fortunate to start in April. I would recommend this for any district leader who knows that a school is in dire straits and there will be new leadership: LET THEM BEGIN BEFORE THE SCHOOL YEAR IS OVER, even if it's for less than a month. That way, you can spend the summer planning what is really needed, and when you walk in the following school year, you can implement what is required to effectively lead the school. When I began in April, on the very first day as the principal of the school, I arrived on the campus lot at about 7:35 a.m. The first bell rang at 8 a.m., so I was only a little early. That's the way I typically operate. I'm not the first one in the building, but I'm usually the last one to leave. I'd rather stay late than get to the campus too early. The first thing I did was drive around the building to try to get a feel for the campus. In order to know where to begin repairing and mending things, my training and experience told me that I first had to simply observe. I observed the most vulnerable parts of the campus, such as areas where kids could easily get out of the building, the student parking lot, the teacher parking lot, and the physical condition of the campus. After I made my round, I parked and just sat in my car. Watching. I think that in many cases, you can figure out a lot more about what's really happening with a building by sitting in the parking lot and observing it in silence, rather than by walking through it and asking people to tell you about what's happening. About 10 minutes before the 8 a.m. bell rang, I made my plea to the Lord; I knew I was about to undertake a huge task, and I would only succeed at it with His covering, guidance, and help. I gathered my things and walked into the building.

Once I entered and got settled in my office, my work of simply observing continued. I observed how timely or tardy the kids were. I observed how the kids transitioned from class to class. I observed what happened when the kids were late to class. I observed the level of urgency of the kids after the bell rang. I counted how many students stood around in the hallway during class. I observed how many kids were on their phones during class (or sleeping), not paying attention to the teacher. I observed how many kids left the campus for lunch (as well as the exit they used to escape) even though we had a closed campus and this was not permissible. I observed the general atmosphere in the hallway. I observed what the kids were wearing and how most of them violated the dress code in some way. I observed what lunch was like.

I also made numerous observations of the teachers, staff, and facility. I observed what the secretaries were doing, how they responded to and greeted parents, and how they managed the check-in and check-out systems. I observed whether or not they made announcements in the morning, who was making the announcements, and what types were made. I stepped into the rooms where professional learning communities (PLCs) were meeting to observe how they were running, who was leading them, and how engaged the teachers were. I observed whether the teachers were on time or not. I observed how many teachers came out into the hallway during the passing periods. I observed how many teachers were at their doors greeting and speaking to the kids as they walked into their classrooms. I observed how teachers responded to students who were late to class. After class began, I observed whether teachers were actually teaching and engaging the students, or if they were sitting down. I observed the building's safety issues, whether the doors were locked at a certain time or whether they remained open for people to get into the building. I observed the cleanliness of the campus and whether or not the custodians were doing their job. More than twenty specific observations. It was my purposeful intent to be overly vigilant.

My work on the first day of the job was just to stand back and assess everything as it was going on in its natural state. I wasn't aloof; I didn't just pass by students and teachers without greeting them. I said hello and exchanged some pleasantries, but my initial work was not to make them think that I was evaluating or coaching them. Now wasn't the time for such things. Now was the time to get a true picture of the school, an authentic understanding of what was happening on the campus with the students, teachers, and staff. If everyone knew I was observing and assessing them, their behavior would have changed, and I would not have gotten an authentic sense of what things were like inside the school. By simply watching without engaging, correcting, or coaching, I was able to develop a clear picture of what I was dealing with on the campus.

After the final school bell rang for the day and students were dismissed, I continued my observation. Now, it was time to get a vision for what the campus was like when there were no guests in the building. People tend to dress things up when people are around. However, when no one is around, they are more inclined to let their guards down, exposing all of the gaps and holes that exist. Those were the very things I needed to see.

It took me about two days to really take everything in, including how the students, teachers, and staff functioned, what was driving the culture, and how the campus operated. I spent the entire first two days on the job, from 8 a.m. until 4:30 p.m., simply observing and making notes, both mental and on my phone. At the end of the day, I would go back and prioritize all of the things that needed to be remedied from most urgent to least urgent, creating a timeline of execution. Of course, my list of notes was an extensive one, and the timeline was short. However, this was no surprise. I took the job knowing that there was a lot that would have to be done, in a short amount of time.

When Dr. Campbell first stepped foot in the door her first year, she made it very clear to students and to her staff as well, "I expect the best out of you, so give me the best that you have to offer!" She knows the students just as well as we know the students, and she's going to push them for greatness. For us as APs, Dr. Campbell doesn't just tell us to be great; she shows us how to be great. She sees your potential. She sees your greatness and sees those things in everyone on this campus, from the teaching staff, to the instructional aide, to the janitor in the cafeteria. She takes these people, and she molds them into being better than the best professional. She invests so much into everyone and has such high expectations of everyone that nobody wants to let her down. She makes everybody truly believe that she believes in them!

- A. Judge, Assistant Principal

Taking Organized Action: The First Year Engagement Phase

After the observation phase came the engagement phase. The fact that I began in my role as principal of the high school in April 2017 meant that I only had about eight weeks to make my mark on the school before the end of the school year in May. Although my observation phase had yielded a long list of requirements that were needed, with limited time before the end of the school year, I decided to focus my efforts on four key areas: (1) establishing structure, (2) ensuring student safety, (3) interpreting data, and (4) increasing student attendance.

> Since 2011, [this campus] has had more administrative turnover than any of Houston's over 40 high schools. The current leader, Khalilah Campbell-Rhone, just finished her first full year and is the school's sixth principal in 10 years.
>
> – Laura Isensee, *Houston Public Media*, News 88.7

Engagement Area 1: Establishing Structure

The most essential starting point in this phase was to bring some organization to the campus. I knew that there needed to be some structure; one of my core beliefs is that without structure, you cannot have a successful campus. I asked the staff for an organizational chart, but it didn't exist. I looked for the campus rules and guidelines, but they were hidden somewhere in the office, and it appeared no one really gave them a second thought. Thus, in my efforts to introduce some structure on the campus, I had to begin with the basics. I put together an organizational chart and began making assignments. This was also the time I began writing the "campus bible" for the school. It would soon include all of the new systems, processes, and procedures that we would begin implementing to bring order to the school.

One of the first systems I implemented was a monitoring system in which I assigned teachers and staff to oversee the campus access points. The goal was to always have someone watching in order to make sure the kids weren't leaving the school before the official dismissal time, sliding under the gates in the back of the building. The monitors also watched the halls to ensure the kids were not in the hallways without a permit, which was something the kids had been accustomed to doing. I also held a faculty meeting where I informed all of the teachers that their kids were not to leave their classrooms without a permit. It was the teacher's responsibility to know exactly where their kids were going at all times. If a student walked out of their class without permission, it was their responsibility to call the front office and say that a kid just walked out of their class without permission.

Even with permission, there were restrictions to when kids could be in the hallways. I implemented a new guideline that did not allow kids to leave out of their class during the first and last 20 minutes of class. There was good reason for this. For the first 20 minutes of class, students should be getting instruction; if they left the class during this time for any reason, after they returned, the teacher would have to re-explain the lesson. During the last 20 minutes, students should be wrapping up their lesson for the day. Only in between the first 20 and the last 20 minutes of class could a student leave the classroom for any reason, and only with a permit.

Of course, it was springtime, testing was upon us, and the natives were restless. Thankfully, I was able to bring in two employees with whom I had previously worked. They were known for their strong sense of discipline in both academics and behavior. As a team, Davis, Judge, and I set guidelines in place in order to get students out of the hallways, which was an essential starting point for engagement. When I began as principal, there would be so many kids in the hallways during class time that a guest visiting the school wouldn't even know that it was class time. Teachers would send their kids to their cars to retrieve their glasses, or something else they'd left behind. Teachers would send their kids to the teacher's lounge to buy them a soda in the middle of class because they were thirsty. Some teachers had even grown accustomed to sending their kids to run general errands to other offices during class time, when the kids should have been learning and working. Consequently, it was critical that we put certain parameters in place to curb all unnecessary hallway activity.

An additional issue that needed more structure was teacher accountability. Teachers would arbitrarily leave campus during their conference period – in the middle of the workday – when they were supposed to be available for parent-teacher conferences, or PLCs. I would look for teachers during their conference period in order to have a word with them, and they were nowhere to be found. After I asked around, I couldn't find anyone who knew (or would tell) where they had gone; they just knew that the teacher didn't seem to be on campus anymore. I had to help the teachers understand that if they didn't ask for permission to leave, and if they didn't sign out when given permission to leave, they were breaking school board policy. This was a *real* job; they could not just leave campus whenever they felt like it. We were still at *work*!

It was quite a culture change. When people started saying that they were simply not aware of the guidelines, we emailed and posted a list of non-negotiables that forbade many of the ways they had been accustomed to operating in the past. For example, if they liked to eat a hot lunch (as I, too, loved to do), they could use the multiple food delivery services that now existed instead of driving several miles away from school, waiting in a long line, and then returning to their class late with a room full of students. Not only would they return to a classroom full of students, but they would also be monitored by me or another staff member, because they were late, and students could not be left unattended. It was now a non-negotiable to send a student to get a beverage for a teacher. It was also a non-negotiable to send a student to their car during class, because this was a huge safety issue, leaving the school susceptible to a great deal of liability. What if something happened to the student in the parking lot while they were going to the teacher's car? Putting a student's safety in jeopardy because of an adult's poor planning would no longer be tolerated.

The bottom line was that the overall school non-negotiable for teachers was doing anything other than teaching during designated class times. For example, I explained that if they needed to get their computer repaired, they had to do so within established set hours. If they needed to turn something into a particular office, the same rule applied. It was a non-negotiable to leave class during class time or send a student to do something for them during class. If they absolutely had to have something brought to them or delivered during class time, they were to find another adult who was available to do it for them, not a student. Also, if they needed to take care of an errand, they needed to do it before school, during lunch, or after school, but not during work hours. Teachers had to be in their assigned places, whether in the classroom, on duty as a monitor when the bell rang, thresholding and saying, "Good morning" to each student when they entered, etc., during work hours. These were the non-negotiables.

We established a few rules – mostly non-negotiables – in the first two-and-a-half weeks of my principalship. I felt that was extremely crucial in establishing structure on the campus. For so long, such rules had not been enforced. If I was going to be there, I needed everyone to understand that effective immediately, we would operate in excellence. Needless to say, the teachers were in shock, and I'm sure they didn't like me. And that was okay; we were still going to follow policy. If not, I would be the one getting the call from the district, and there was no time to field those calls because we needed to work on academics and help our students succeed. The bottom line was that kids were going to be in class during class time because they were there to learn. Teachers needed to be in their classrooms during the workday because they were there to teach.

A few times, we had to write teachers up for rule violations, because they continued to go against policy, doing things we'd clearly said we were no longer going to do. That's when the majority of the teachers recognized that I wasn't just talking; I was serious. They knew that although they had new leaders in the past who'd tried to implement new standards, policies, and procedures on campus, those leaders had slowly been worn down by some of the teachers' determined non-compliance. Now, the immediate write-ups for violating the guidelines and safety standards of our school caused the teachers to listen a little more carefully and become more serious about adhering to the newly established campus policies. Let me be clear, I supported my teachers to the fullest, but we could not operate in mediocrity and say we wanted what's best for kids.

Engagement Area 2: Ensuring Student Safety

Another big culture change that had to be introduced on the campus, almost immediately, was restructuring our security system in order to ensure the safety and well-being of the students. Safety was not a minute issue; it was serious. For example, right before I became principal, there was a drive-through (no shots were fired) on the campus. A group of guys drove onto our campus parking lot during the school day, brandishing weapons and hanging out of their car windows. Apparently, they had an issue with one of the students in the school. However, my first question wasn't who their beef was with; it was, "Who was on duty, and why wasn't the gate closed after the morning bell?" This was an incident that could have been avoided by following proper safety protocols.

Establishing some of the necessary safety protocols on the campus did not come without struggle. For instance, when we tried to ensure that our campus gates were closed after school began in the mornings, we got pushback from the city for safety reasons. Their argument was that we couldn't close the gates because we didn't have a separate entrance and egress. I stood my ground, making my own argument for the safety of my students. I asked lots of challenging questions: "How am I supposed to keep my campus safe if you're telling me that I can't close the gates? How am I going to keep people from driving onto our parking lot if I can't lock the gates? Is the city going to send additional security for our campus to keep the kids safe?" In the end, they sent out several police sergeants to see how we could secure the campus parking lot while ensuring that safety vehicles could effectively enter our lot. We settled on closing one gate and keeping another open, ensuring that people could not simply drive onto the campus during the school day. That was a good day!

The campus already had district police officers assigned to it. When I first arrived, the officers shared information of how things had been on the campus. They were definitely on board but wanted the culture to change, as well as to be mentors for the students. They were pained when their job went from monitoring and mentoring to arresting. My position was that it was better to be proactive rather than reactive, and they were game! My APs were super tough, which made the load they were accustomed to carrying much lighter. We all agreed that not every issue was a police issue. I believe that the students were amazed that none of us "new folks" (and at that time, it was an all-female administrative team), were afraid to do anything, and for that, we quickly gained the respect of the students.

We were all assigned to make regular sweeps of the restrooms every 10 to 15 minutes throughout the school day, so the kids couldn't sneak away and do things un-monitored in these areas. I wanted the officers to be highly visible so that the kids would see them and think twice about doing things that they shouldn't. Raising the profile of our campus officers and putting extra safety parameters in place helped to cut down on a lot of unacceptable activities that had been taking place on the campus for years.

Our relationships with the students proved to be imperative at this time. Many of my former students would put the word out, but there would always be non-believers. One day, while returning from lunch with the students, a teacher stood at her door, barely whispering my name. When I made it close enough to hear her, my attention was averted by the movement of desks. Two young men were going at it like Tyson versus Holyfield! I negotiated when I would jump into the fight, ensuring I could protect my belly. As I decided to move in closer, a student came from behind me, lifted me up and out of the way and said, "Back up Dr. Campbell, I got this!" Trying to regain my balance, another young man jumped in on the other side, and just like that, the fight was over, and the young man who had 'saved' me was admonishing Tyson and Holyfield for fighting in front of the principal. Although I would never advocate a student breaking up a fight, EVER, he beat me to the punch (literally). He was a former student of mine and he knew I did not tolerate the nonsense. Once the students saw that we meant business, they joined in. They needed the stress of being in an unsafe school alleviated from their shoulders. They deserved a safe haven and a viable learning environment.

The various changes that I made to the way that the teachers and staff operated weren't always received with enthusiasm. I'll admit that these immediate changes were big adjustments to the campus operations. Some might even call these changes "drastic." Educational administrators tend to advise that when you go into a new environment, you shouldn't go in making rapid changes. I agree. I subscribe to the thought that changes should be gradually and systematically implemented. However, when it comes to matters as urgent as student safety and instruction, I think exceptions apply. In these areas, I believe that it's necessary to go in and make immediate changes, putting systems in place to ensure that kids are where they are supposed to be, when they are supposed to be there, so that they can learn and remain out of harm's way.

Dr. Campbell understood the obstacles that hindered student achievement. Not just what was written, researched, and studied, but she understood those intangible things that were integral to the ever-growing quagmire embedded in schools across the nation. Her "compassion" for disenfranchised children propelled her to lead with her heart not with the educational buzzwords of the day. The "courage" to defy is my link to this amazing administrator. Do what's best, check your ego at the door. That's how I teach, that's how she leads.

Without these crucial attributes, how can anyone lead? She has repeatedly employed these pivotal concepts when moving schools out of unacceptable status. This high school is just the last of Dr. Campbell's impressive achievements. Giving teachers the latitude to inspire using previous life experiences and trusting them to forge new paths that led to student self-realization which in turn led to students thirsting for knowledge. This is what sets her apart. No one seems to trust this practice anymore. She depends on it. All of the schools she has worked in or led are proof positive that these qualities prevail in education. Without leaders like Dr. Campbell, teachers and staff would simply become corporate yes-men. Yes, "corporate." Isn't that where education is heading? Well, thankfully not here.

– M. Judge, Math Specialist

Engagement Area 3: Analyzing Data

The third critical area of engagement that was of great necessity at the high school was that of knowing where our students were in terms of learning and being prepared for the End of Course Assessments. By the end of my first week on the job, I began going over data with the teachers. This was a critical and immediate area that needed to be addressed, because when we asked teachers how many of their kids were in danger of not passing the end-of-course STAAR exam, they had no idea. I was so baffled! I thought, *It's the end of the year, and you're only two weeks away from testing! How have you been teaching these students all semester and not know whether or not they're on target to pass or fail?* It seemed as if they were just throwing concepts up into the air and seeing whether they would land with the students or not. They weren't targeting their efforts in any particular direction. They were just going through the motions, never checking whether or not they were actually headed in the right direction. This was when I had them pull out the data, and I sat down with them to review and analyze it.

What's worse, there were some teachers who had been out for up to two months, and they were just returning to school. Their classes had either been split among their fellow content colleagues, or they'd had a substitute teaching their class. Still, no one had been monitoring the fact that these teachers had been out, the impact that their absence would have on their kids, and whether their kids had the knowledge they needed to pass the STAAR test. It was bewildering to me that some teachers were not monitoring the progress of these kids, especially considering that this was a school that was in danger of being shut down due to lack of performance!

Unfortunately, despite my efforts to teach the teachers how to analyze the data, time was too far gone for these exercises to have a huge impact on the STAAR results. At that point, there was nothing we could do to go back and fix the fact that the kids had not been prepared to take the test. Still, because I knew that if anyone had plans to return the next school year, they needed to learn how to read and analyze data. All we did was work on data for those last couple of months. We taught them how to collect data, how to read and analyze data, and how to use the data to drive instruction, rather than just shooting in the dark. I was aware that when it was all said and done, the school might not benefit from them learning these skills. After all, school was practically over for the year, and they might not be working at the school in the upcoming year. However, I thought it was my responsibility to empower them with this skill, so that if they returned, they were ready to hit the ground running!

Engagement Area 4: Increasing Student Attendance

The next big area that I had to address, after getting students out of the hallways and into the classrooms, ensuring their safety on campus and charting a path to graduation through analyzing data, was the attendance issue. There were so many kids that should have been going to school on our campus who did not. Either they didn't come to school at all, or they would come to school and then leave at some point during the day. Both of these types of absences were unacceptable to me. For the students who skipped a ton of school, they were in danger of not graduating and/or completely dropping out of school. For the students who left campus before the end of the school day, they were in danger of not earning enough credits to graduate. Besides this, there were safety issues with leaving early. If a student left school early and as a result, was injured, we would be held partially responsible. In light of this, I had to put systems in place to get students into the school, then put additional systems into place to ensure that they didn't get out before the final bell rang for the day.

The first thing I did was implement a system of accountability for taking attendance. As soon as I began my observations, I quickly learned that teachers were not taking attendance properly in their classrooms. As a result, the office was never properly informed that students were absent or skipping, so students' parents were never made aware that their kids were absent until it was too late to catch them in the act of skipping. Thus, we had to ensure that attendance was actually being *taken* properly by the teachers. We began holding them accountable for posting their attendance for every class period. These were key adjustments necessary in order for the next piece of the puzzle, our campus call-out system, to work effectively.

The campus call-out system was a system that called parents to let them know that their child was marked absent if the student was not recorded present in any specific period. If a student was absent for one, two or three days, the parents would receive an automated call from the system notifying them of the child's absence. On the second day of the student being absent, the parents received a call from an actual person. I should note that this was the process we put into place when I first began — the last couple of months of 2017. It was the end of the school year, there were so many changes to be made in so many areas, and there were *a countless number* of student absences. Although I strongly believe in having a person from the office call parents when their children are absent, we simply didn't have the manpower to call all of the parents of students who had been missing for one day. However, the following year, starting with the fall 2018 semester, I would go on to change the system so that parents would receive a call from an actual person from the office on the *very first* day their child was absent.

As it turned out, a lot of the kids had just been getting by with staying home because their parents left for work early in the morning and never saw whether they went to school or not. Since the parents weren't receiving phone calls saying that their kids were absent, they assumed that their kids had been at school! Simply knowing that their parents would be notified if they were not marked present in class led students to go to class.

I thought it was important for parents to play a role in ensuring that their children were at school. We would call them and ask, "Hi, we are looking for Mr. or Mrs. XYZ? Did you know your child was absent?" Sometimes, they would say that they knew their child was not at school; sometimes they were sick, and other times, they would have doctor's appointments. As long as they knew their child was absent and had a reason, fine. However, if they said that they didn't know their child wasn't at school, we would spring into action and try to find the child. This would begin with a phone call to the child asking, "Where are you?" "Where have you been?" "Why aren't you at school?" Sometimes, when we would talk to the students, we would find that there were issues other than simply not wanting to come to school at play. For example, most of our kids either walked or took the city bus to school. When it was raining hard or if it was really cold, they tended to not want to come to school because of the inconvenience of being exposed to these elements, either from walking or having to stand at one or more bus stops. When we found that this was the case, we would contact parents and work out arrangements to get students to school.

One of the most innovative ways that we used to reduce skipping and increase our attendance during my first year (April and May of 2017) was to hop into a golf cart and ride around the neighborhood, including apartment complexes in our neighborhood. These were areas that no one would have ever ridden through before, because, as I've mentioned, it was deemed unsafe. However, there was too much at stake for us to sit within the four walls of the school and be afraid. Our kids were missing in action, and we had to go get them. Our mindset was that if these were our kids, we couldn't be afraid of the area; there was no way that we could effectively serve the kids that we served all day long if we were afraid to go into the neighborhoods in which they lived.

With this in mind, we would hop on our little red golf cart and ride through the neighborhood, sometimes for an hour or two. We'd roll through, honking the horn and waving at the parents and community members. They'd be sitting outside, and we'd pull up to them and hand them our business card, introducing ourselves. Then, we'd tell them to call us if they ever saw one of our kids hanging out during the time that they should be in school, and we'd come pick them up. When they heard this, they would be so astonished. They typically replied, "Really? Are you serious? We've never seen *anything* like this before!" Seeing our commitment led them to become engaged with the campus. Since they saw us putting in the effort, they wanted to do their part to ensure the students' success, working as our partners to get our kids to school. They became our eyes and ears on the ground —informants that helped us know where to go to find our kids.

Sometimes, we would ride around to see which kids we could find just hanging out. Once we found them, we would call for transportation and take them to the school. Other times, the people in the community would call us and tell us that some of our kids were sitting behind their house skipping school, smoking, or just hanging out. In fact, any time they saw anyone who looked like a high school-aged kid and not on campus during the school day, they would assume the kid was ours, and I would call out on the radio that I was riding. Sometimes, someone wanted to join. It was usually Assistant Principal Judge or Assistant Principal Davis, but many times others wanted to experience the ride. I often giggle when I think how later we discovered the kids would record us on Snapchat riding the golf cart, unbeknownst to us, and it would spread like wildfire that we were 'riding.'

Engagement Area 5: Establishing a Community Presence

We really tried to establish a presence in the community during my first few months at the school, so that people would know that there was a new team in town, and that we were serious about what we were doing. If you asked the school district and community, they would say that we were successful in this effort. By the end of my first year, even though it only lasted for a couple of months, we had made a significant impact. Everyone associated with the school knew we had established a no-nonsense culture: a team had come into the community to finally bring real change and transformation to the school they loved.

These processes, procedures, and systems only represent a small sampling of what was done at the school in order to bring some immediate order to the campus that was desperately in need of structure, organization, safety, instructional direction, and student attrition. However, these examples should help with understanding the essential areas that may need to be addressed as priorities in order to begin a similar turnaround and transformation process.

Chapter 3
Transformational Leadership Tips

TLT 3.1
Make Your Commitment Clear to Yourself and Your Loved Ones

- There will be many moments of happiness, but there will also be sacrifices. Be prepared for the highs and lows and ensure those closest to you are ready as well.

TLT 3.2
Commit for the Right Reason

- During the most difficult times of the turnaround, the only thing that will keep you focused and sustain you is your "why" – your reason for embarking upon such a difficult challenge. In light of this, be sure that you commit to the work for a strong, compelling reason.

TLT 3.3
Look Before You Leap Into Making Changes

- Once you commit to a campus, do not go in and just begin making changes. Instead, take the time to observe and learn the strengths and weaknesses of a campus before you make substantial changes. Unless of course, there are major safety or instructional issues – still make them with careful call. But keep in mind, everything can't wait – safety is your top priority!

TLT 3.4
Be Smart About the Need

- Be smart about defining what the need is and what the plan is. Conquer your most arduous tasks first – they are usually the most important!

- Define non-negotiables and stick to them. Systems make life so much easier.

4

The Summertime Shake-up

Starting from Scratch to Build and Inspire a Winning Team

I began the summer after my first year as principal of the high school feeling immense joy! My elation was not just grounded in the relief that the school year was over, and I had survived my first—although very short—year as the principal, my indescribable mood was cemented in the measurable results that we'd already produced around culture, in such a short amount of time. There was new life growing inside of me and new life budding on campus. I wanted everything to be perfect when school began, whether I was there or out on maternity leave.

Considering what we had been able to accomplish with the existing teachers and staff, I could only *imagine* the leaps and bounds toward transformation that would be made with a winning team! Throughout my career as a transformational leader, I've found that the biggest key to success is being able to hand-pick the ideal team. A team comprised of educators that have both the skills and the passion to do the work. I always use this question as a driving force: do they have the will and the skill? I can coach up a skill, but I can't teach will; that is something my team members must already possess. The students who attended the school and the community that loved the legendary institution deserved a team that was qualified and committed to giving the students their best. I was determined to put together such a team that would help the school and community (both of which had grown accustomed to losing) score a huge win.

It shouldn't come as a surprise that many teachers quit over the summer. They jumped ship, and that spoke volumes! In many ways, I expected this to happen for two main reasons. First, we only had one year to turn the high school around and bring it up to acceptable status. Considering the school's losing track record over the past, it was hard to be optimistic about its future. Even with a new leader in place as principal, there was no assurance that if they stayed with the school for the upcoming school year, they would have a job at the end of it. Why should they believe that this new principal would be able to do the impossible? Unless she had some kind of superpowers, there was no way she'd be able to make it happen, either. Therefore, believing that the high school was just too far behind to be turned around in one year, even with a new leader at the helm, they said their goodbyes and found other jobs.

The second reason was because they'd gotten a taste of what my leadership was like during the last two months of the school year in April and May of 2017. They knew that if it wasn't good for kids, it wouldn't be tolerated. Period. There would no longer be such a thing as doing a job halfway at this school; everything had to be done with 110% effort, or it would be labeled as "unacceptable." The rumor was that, under my leadership, teachers would have to work harder, work longer, work smarter, know their stuff, be overly prepared, and be meticulously organized. Gone were the days of being a subpar teacher at this beloved institution; everything was about to change. Those who weren't willing to function in such a demanding environment, abandoning their non-results driven (and comfortable) mindset, knew it was time to find their calling somewhere else. To those who were ready and able, I said, "Let's get to work!"

Hiring Challenge 1: Inviting Star Assistant Principals to Win

As soon as I began operating in my position as principal, I already knew it was a must to surround myself with like-minded assistant principals who were hungry to win and would support my winning vision. It was time to get on the phone and make some calls.

I began the assistant principal hiring process by calling in educators that I had formed solid relationships with, both professionally and personally, over the years. These were exceptional leaders who had worked with me previously. They had proven track records of success, and not just with kids that came from affluent homes, but with kids that looked like the kids on my campus. The recipients of my phone calls were true professionals who were experienced in producing successful students in tough environments. They had both intellect and grit; they were built for this challenge. Best of all, by reaching out to people who were familiar with leading in spaces like the one this high school occupied, I didn't have to do a lot of explaining; they already knew the challenges we'd be up against.

Asking these people to leave the stability of their current jobs and come to work with me at the school as assistant principals was both difficult and risky. If they left the comfort, familiarity, and stability of their current jobs to join me, and we failed at successfully turning the school around, they would be jobless in a year, because the campus would be closed; the district would be requested to wipe everybody out, from the principal to the custodian, and place them elsewhere. Coming to this school and failing could potentially end with a blemish on their resume, and possibly damage their career. Thus, asking people to leave their jobs and come to work with me, with the full knowledge of these potentials, was difficult for me to do. However, I also knew that by bringing in heavy hitters like the ones I personally called was the only way that we were going to make transformational change on the campus. With these people—the right people—on my team as assistant principals, I was fully confident that we could turn the campus around in one year. They were all part of *The Formula*.

Even before I began putting together my dream team of assistant principals, I knew it wasn't going to be a quick and simple task. I didn't expect them to jump at the opportunity without a second thought. Just as I'd had to take time to consider things, jump through a lot of hurdles, and talk myself over a number of obstacles in order to bring myself to accept my position, I knew that it might take some convincing for others to join the team. Educators from all over the district were familiar with the school's reputation, so it wasn't going to be easy to get them to the campus. However, I knew that the key to getting them to say "Yes" would be in helping them to understand that joining this team would be worth it, and that I would give them everything I had to coach, train, and lead them to success.

What I didn't say to the educators that I called in to serve as assistant principals on my team was, "I only need you for a year because there's a strong chance you won't have a job a year from now." What I did say to them was this:

"I know that this is a big career change to come to this campus. I also know it's a risky move. But what I need you to know is that the students

are suffering here, and they deserve better. They need people like you to come over, genuinely care about them, and lead them. I know you and your abilities, and I know that you can succeed. I'm putting together an all-star team, and together, we can turn this school around. I just need you to say "Yes," believe in these kids, and believe in me to lead you to the finish line. I assure you that I can do this, but I can't do it without you."

After I shared my sentiments with them, I told them to think about it, hung up the phone, and waited. Fortunately, all of the individuals that I personally invited called back and said, "Yes!" After this, I got on the phone with their principals and negotiated to allow them to leave. Within the next month, we had a complete administrative team: my hand-picked dream team!

So, who were these hand-picked individuals, and what was I thinking when I chose them? Each person that I chose had an impeccable skill set, and each skill set matched what my assessment said I needed. I began sifting through my brain like it was an old school Rolodex. By this point, my first thoughts landed on those who had once worked with me. The only challenge was that most of them were principals now. I continued to think, and I landed on Davis (whom I discussed in Chapter 3). She was a no-nonsense disciplinarian working at a local middle school in a teacher capacity, but I had worked with her before, and I knew she'd be able to help me gain control of the environment. I was able to bring her on board before the end of April 2017 when I first took on the principal position at the school. The principal of the middle school she was working at, who was also one of my colleagues, supported the decision to allow her to promote schools in April rather than making her wait until the end of the school year to take the new job working with me. Although bringing people on to a new job position in the middle of the school year was not district practice or a common approach that we took as principals, my colleagues leaned in to help in any way possible.

Next was my double threat, Assistant Principal Judge. I was able to snag her early; I mentioned her in Chapter 3 as well. Not only did she have an amazing culture-building personality, but she knew science like no one's business. I like to refer to her as our personal Josephine Silone Yates (a famous, history-making African American female educator and activist who fought for racial and social change)! What was even more of a blessing, was the fact that I was able to onboard her father, Mr. Judge, who is the most masterful math teacher I've ever met in my life. We'd been working together for the past 10 years, only to be separated by my one year as a school support officer. I hired him at the very first high school that was set to be closed in 2008, and he kicked some serious academic butt there! When I transitioned to principal at the middle school level, I brought him along. Now, the opportunity presented itself for us to be reunited once more while working together on this campus. Not only was this a massive win for me, but I knew how much the students would benefit from his skill set and relationship-building skills. Let me remind you of something: I did not only want to build a team that would ensure a significant shift in scores and data; we needed a team that would positively alter the culture, morale, and mindset of our kids.

My next two hires were two heavy hitters. (Yes, you read that right; two more hires! I was fortunate enough to hire four administrators, since the previous ones, with the exception of one, were no longer at the school.) Heavy hitter number 1: Hampton, aka "T. Hamp." She was smart and quick witted. Since she had already been a high school assistant principal, she clearly had all the characteristics that were needed for the position. She was well versed in the areas of student credits, grade transfers, attendance criteria, rules and regulations, master scheduling, and our SIS (Student Information System), just to name a few. With her on the team, I would be able to leverage her expertise to build capacity within my other two assistant principals. I had hired her eight years prior to oversee special education at the high school level, and now, she was a guru.

My second heavy hitter: Dotson. He was a mixture of an FBI agent, MacGyver, and Einstein! I had known him since college and worked with him for years, but most importantly, I trusted him with my life. I pulled him in as an assistant principal whose specific purpose was to oversee student discipline, implement systems and structures, and ensure all students were safe on our campus. He naturally thought like an agent but genuinely loved kids. That was what we needed on the campus.

Once I had all the team members on board that I knew could do the work (including Jefferson—the one former assistant principal that was previously there), the real labor and training began. It was imperative that I brief everyone on secondary guidelines and show them how things functioned in a high school. It was our goal to maintain a laser-like focus on all-around campus excellence.

Hiring Challenge 2: Identifying Coachable, Qualified Teachers

With some of the best assistant principals in Texas now working on my team, it was time to open up hiring to qualified teachers who wanted to apply. It was the beginning of summer, and we were tasked with replacing quite a few teachers before the new school year began in the fall. This was not something new to me; I'd been in the position before of having to hire a multitude of teachers in a short period of time. We had to be strategic when interviewing prospects, because working at this school was going to be a unique experience. Strategically balancing reality and inspiration so that candidates would have a clear picture of what they were signing up for (if they were offered the position) was crucial.

Dr. Campbell has a knack for hiring the right people for the right job! Even when I took this position on, I had to have a conversation with my husband. I was like, "Okay, I'm gonna go work for Campbell, so you know it's going to be long hours and weekends." He said, "Whatever you've got to do! She's going to push you so that the school is great, but you're also great as well!" He was right. Dr. Campbell wants to succeed, but she wants you to be successful, too.

- T. Hampton, Assistant Principal

Being the smart educators that they were, a lot of the candidates who applied to work at our school did their research beforehand. They googled our school and read what the media had to say about us before the interview. Then, they would call us and say, "Well, you know… you guys are just really too far for me." We were not naïve; we knew the school wasn't too far. They were concerned about their safety and job security. If they couldn't provide support with getting our school turned around, they would be looking for another job at the same time next year.

Other candidates would arrive early to drive around the surrounding neighborhood before coming to their interview. By the time they came into the interview room with us, they would have a look on their face that showed they were already in fear for their lives. We knew we would never see nor hear from those candidates again; on a campus like ours, a teacher could show no fear.

Then, there were the brave ones. They also drove through the neighborhood on the way to their interview, but instead of looking fearful, they came in with boldness. We would ask them, "Do you know where you are?" They would assure us that they knew exactly where they were, and that they were ready for the challenge. When interviewing the candidates who actually showed for the interview, we would always begin with outlining the expectations of what teaching at our school would look like. I would very honestly say to them in what I call the "let me tell you up front" conversation:

"Look, let me be up front. This is not your typical school, and these are not your typical kids. This is a tough school. If you're not cut out for toughness, you're not going to like it here. Uncomfortable situations may occur in your classroom, and they may happen frequently. You have to be able to handle yourself in this environment, because it's not for the faint at heart. However, in spite of what surrounds them, you should know that the kids in this school are loving, very intelligent, hardworking, and they're ready for someone who's going to get before them and do the job that has to be done. They're capable learners, and they need teachers that believe in them.

I'll be frank, in order to teach here, you're going to have to work longer hours than normal. However, I'm willing to compensate you for the extra time. It's also going to be emotionally taxing because our students come with issues— issues that would provoke most adults to want to go into a corner to cry. But you've got to be able to hear their issues, sympathize with them, and teach them, because at the end of the day, the only thing that's going to help get them out of any situation they're in, is having a good education. If you're going to empathize with them so much that you lower the standard of expectation for them, you're not doing them any good. So, first of all, be very honest with yourself, and tell me if you can endure this environment, because if you can't, we need to stop the interview right now."

There were some people who were like, "Thank you for your honesty. No, this is not the place for me." They left the interview and never called us again. I can appreciate that. I can deal with that. What I can't deal with is people not knowing themselves enough to know what they can and can't handle, only to take the job and quit in the middle of the school year because they underestimated what they thought it would take to teach our students. If I got a green light from the candidate after the "let me tell you up front" conversation, we started the interview.

One day, when we had taken hit after hit in the hiring process, a young man came in, sat down and waited outside my office to be interviewed. We perused his resume and noticed that he had no teaching experience. I think we slithered down in our chairs simultaneously. We wanted to make at least one good hire that day, and we didn't feel like the odds were in our favor. I peeked outside my door, and there sat a young man who appeared small in stature. "Let's hurry up and interview so we can go home!" I told Assistant Principal Judge.

In walked Mr. Nguyen. He had the firmest handshake of anyone that we'd interviewed thus far. He looked me dead in my eyes and stated his name. His voice commanded my attention, and he kept strong posture throughout the interview. During the next hour, we learned that he was a 2nd Dan in Tae Kwon Do and could cook a mean meal. Most importantly, he knew the sciences – chemistry and physics – like no one's business. Mr. Nguyen went on to be an amazing teacher who wasn't afraid to pick up rodents with his bare hands and drop eggs from the second floor for physics experiments. While on a field trip with students, a wayward driver ran into the bus that followed the one he was on. He jumped off of his bus and ran through traffic (while on the cell phone with me) to ensure that all students and teachers were uninjured and safe. They were about 40 miles out of town when the accident occurred. He remained there as the point person until I arrived. The moral of the story: never judge a book by its cover. To this day, Mr. Nguyen is an amazing teacher.

Success Factor 1: Do They Know Their Stuff?

The very first thing I sought to understand about candidates was whether they had the knowledge base for the particular subject they were applying for. We discerned this by having them do a mini lesson during the interview.

A lot can be observed about candidates when they do the mini lesson. For example, I can tell how nervous they're going to be in front of the kids, how practical and engaging they are with their teaching style, how well they connect with their audience, and whether they know the content. However, the two most important skills any candidate needs are: (1) relationship building skills and (2) content knowledge. If they know content and can construct solid, authentic relationships, they are coachable in other areas. Without these two critical skills, it is tremendously hard for any educator to be successful.

If you are asking questions and the person does not respond correctly, ask them in a different way. If they continue to not respond favorably, they may not be the right person for your campus need. Ask questions. Lots of questions. This is your opportunity to get to know this person, as well as possible, in a short amount of time.

Success Factor 2: Can They Relate to the Kids?

After identifying a candidate's content knowledge, the next thing we looked for was personality, and whether or not they were relatable. If they didn't have good people skills, they weren't going to be able to do a good job with our kids. Period! On our campus (and probably at every campus in the world), nine times out of ten, students were going to work harder for the teacher if they liked the teacher. However, if the kids didn't like the teacher, they would shut down, fail to do the work, and refuse to learn.

The best candidate for a campus like ours was a personable, energetic, and quick-witted one. This is important in any candidate because they will have to be able to banter back and forth with the kids in a fun and loving manner. Without the ability to do this, kids will assume they can get over on a teacher. At that point, the teacher is done with; it's over! Personality also determines whether or not a teacher is going to be able to negotiate with the surroundings of the school. I can't emphasize enough how important it was to have personality at a school like ours. Even when teachers are brand new to a campus, have no teaching experience, but have the content knowledge, coupled with the right personality, they are an asset to you and the vision.

Another aspect of being relatable is the ability to remain current and stay abreast of what's happening in our students' worlds (or at least being somewhat invested in the lives of the kids). This applies to all teachers—older, younger, or in-between. Without knowing what's happening with the kids, including the language they are speaking, the colloquialisms they are using, what's going on in pop culture, music, entertainment, social media, etc., teachers won't be able to make a connection with them.

I've been asked about whether I believe teachers and staff who do not look like the kids we serve at our school can still relate to the students in such a way that they are able to successfully engage and educate them. Some people assume that in order to be relatable to kids who live in the inner city, an educator would have to be able to relate based on being of the same demographic or having experienced the same kind of upbringing. I'm sure that looking like and being raised like our students might pay a part in how students initially respond to the educators that serve them. However, I think that what outweighs a similar look or upbringing is heart and investment—whether the educator wants to win with the kids or not—that makes a bigger difference. I have had some phenomenal teachers of different races. I mean, *phenomenal.* Our students adored them and were heartbroken when they couldn't follow them year after year. I've also had some that did not work out, but the ratio was similar to having Black teachers of a similar background that did not work either. Consequently, I don't believe the ability to relate and engage with kids has to do purely with race. I think it has much more to do with how much a person is willing to dig in, get to know the kids, and meet their needs. Kids are simply looking for love, care, and concern; they want to know that someone is always looking out for them, and that the person has their back. Although the teacher may be looked upon as an outsider in the beginning, at the end of it all, kids don't care about gender, color, or race. All that matters is they know they are genuinely cared about.

For instance, I had a new teacher coach who was a white female. The kids adored her. They looked for her all day long, because she purposely made it a point to learn their names and build relationships with them. While observing students transition after the first period bell one morning, I overheard a conversation she was having with a student.

"Hey, I didn't see you yesterday. I missed you. Where've you been?"

"Miss, you were *looking* for me?"

With a smile on her face, she replied, "Of course, I was. You're my favorite!"

She would share parts of her life with them, and in turn, she wanted to know about them and their lives. The kids would say things to her like, "Miss, you're white. You'd never understand." She'd quickly respond, "I'd never understand what? I'd never understand poverty? I'd never understand bad times?" Then, she would give the run down on the things she'd been through in life that mirrored some of the kids' own struggles. The kids would be shocked, and attitudes would change.

When people are willing to give a piece of themselves and willing to find that relatable space between themselves and the student, that's where true connection occurs. The relationships she built with the students were amazing. Her example was the kind of relationship building that trust with kids is built on. The fact that she didn't look like the kids didn't matter; the connection she created with them was authentic, and that's what mattered most of all.

Success Factor 3: Are They Willing to Go the Extra Mile?

Teachers must be totally invested in working on a turnaround campus, because it's not an easy assignment. Everything was "extra" at our school. Not only are the kids going to be dealing with challenges in their home life that are going to make teaching a challenge, but they are teenagers. Their lives are filled with drama! Teens are naturally going to need a lot of time and attention, but those who grow up in environments like the one surrounding our school need it at another level. You must come prepared to deal with teenagers and their crises. They need extra instruction, extra counseling, extra patience, extra time with helping them settle conflicts and beefs with their peers, extra time understanding what's appropriate and inappropriate social behavior; everything is *extra*. Teachers must possess the ability to both empathize with what the kids are going through, and still teach them so they meet and exceed academic benchmarks. In a nutshell, you have to come prepared to meet students where they are, and get them where they need to be, both in academics and life. Many of the teachers at our school had dual roles as cheerleading coaches, dance team instructors, robotics teachers, UIL instructors, band directors, etc. So, when I say, "Extra mile," I mean it.

Success Factor 4: Are They Coachable?

Teachers must be coachable. They must have the ability to receive guidance and direction and modify their behavior according to the coaching they receive. To try to assess the candidates' levels of coachability, we asked questions like, "When is the last time you failed? Who coached you through success after that failure?" Then, we listened very carefully to their answers. We listened to understand how participatory they were in the coaching process. This is because although you can be coached by the best coach, if you're not willing to dig your feet in and make things happen yourself, or you're not dedicated to making a change, you're not going to get any better.

Although everyone on a team receives coaching at some level, some fundamental skills and knowledge should be in place from the very beginning, in order to minimize the amount of coaching necessary to make a teacher successful. Some key points to consider when coaching teachers:

- Plan for kids who are academically lower than expected.

- Design a plan for kids who are more academically advanced—differentiate the learning in order to keep them engaged and ahead.

- Strategize a plan of action for excessively disruptive students—have expectations, rules, and consequences in place, along with a rewards system (to incentivize students), and a plan for students with disabilities.

These are smaller key points to focus on, and are tremendously easy to coach around, but the teacher will have to have a certain *je ne sais quoi*—the personality that allows you to relate to, connect to, and succeed with the kids—on their own.

Of course, these success factors didn't represent a comprehensive list of what we looked for in the best possible candidates to work at our school. There were also other things, like stability, for example. If you see that the candidate has moved from campus to campus often, that's an issue. It's not only an issue because it may suggest a person's inability to remain focused and committed to a position, but it is a larger issue because at a school like ours, kids needed stability. When students' lives are filled with instability, we need school to be the place where they can come and know what was there yesterday will still be there the next day—something stable, predictable, and consistent.

**

Over the summer, leading into the fall 2018 semester, we interviewed a lot of people. A *lot*! The sheer number of candidates that we interviewed allowed us to meet some top talent. We were able to sit back and assess if they would fit our school's mold. There were some candidates who were bright, sharp, experienced, and very knowledgeable. Any school would love to have them and bring them onto their teaching staff. However, they weren't a good fit for *our* campus. Because of this, we passed on a lot of what would be considered *really* good talent to other campuses. Although they had the abilities to teach, we knew they wouldn't do well on a campus like ours.

Although many of these candidates had been teaching for years and were excellent on paper, they had worked at campuses where most of the students were close to, at, or above their standard grade level proficiencies. This would not be the reality at our school. Remember, our kids were sometimes up to five grade levels below where they should have been. That meant, for example, that our science teachers would not have the luxury of simply teaching science; they would simultaneously have to teach the kids comprehension, as a process, in order for them to be able to *under-stand* the science content and learn the lesson! Hearing good reading early on at home (and at school), as well as engaging in read and think-alouds, are just a few things that would have helped mitigate this deficit. Added to this were the classroom discipline issues on a level that teachers who had taught at more mainstream campuses had never experienced before and would likely not be able to handle. It takes a special kind of person to have both the knowledge base, the willingness, and ability to exercise the level of patience necessary to impart their knowledge to kids who have so many odds stacked against them.

We get it: our kids were completely different to teach. They weren't (and are not) difficult to love. They weren't (and are not) difficult to be around. They weren't (and are not) even difficult to discipline. It was a challenge, however, to reach them academically. This is exactly why, during the hiring process, even those who had strong content knowledge and experience were not guaranteed a spot on our team. It took so much more to win at a school like ours. When we found the teachers that had the full package *and* were a good fit for a campus like ours, they made the list of finalists.

Hiring Challenge 3: Getting the Right Teachers with the Right Fit in the Right Places

I believe one of the best parts of what we did during our hiring process was to interview and hire in teams. For example, the assistant principal who was over the science department participated in the interviews scheduled for science candidates. For the most part, that assistant principal made the final decision about which candidates to select. Why did I allow them to make the final choice? Because if the person did not work out, the weight of the decision was going to fall on that assistant principal's shoulders. Remember: all of my assistant principals oversaw subject areas that they could teach (and coach) themselves. Therefore, as we went to interview the candidates together, I prepared the assistant principals by saying:

We're all going to conduct these interviews as a group. We're all going to provide our final feedback on the candidate. However, the final decision of who to hire in your department is up to you. If the people that you hire don't work out, you're going to have to go into their classroom and teach/supervise the class until you find another qualified person, and finding good talent takes time. Unless you want to become a part-time classroom teacher again, pay attention, and pick the right candidates who are ready to do the job. Make sure that in this hiring process, you're selecting people who have the subject knowledge, who have the personality, are in it for the long haul, willing to receive coaching and guidance, able to put in the extra hours, determined to stay the course with the kids, incredibly organized, and who will have really good classroom management.

Typically, during the interview process, we allotted about 30 minutes to pick up on if a candidate possessed the essential qualities, or success factors, that were needed to succeed at a school like ours. This is the hardest part of the hiring process. Most of the time, when you go with your collective gut, you hire the right teachers, who are the right fit, for the right positions. Everything works out just fine.

For example, I hired my assistant principal over science to solely focus on the science department, with a specific concentration on biology. Our biology scores were the scores that counted for accountability on the STAAR test. I did the same thing with every other subject, with a laser-like focus on the ones that would help us in each area measured on the STAAR test. I also hired someone (Dotson) to exclusively deal with the culture of the school, and the discipline of the students. He was the right person for this role. To say he did a good job would be an insult. He did a phenomenal job. We cut down the number of campus fights by nearly fifty percent! We hired people to have a keen focus on exactly what we needed to make happen. It was a winning team. One that would go on to help us accomplish what others deemed impossible to do in one year.

Not everyone who began on the team won with the team. This is because, in the hiring process, some people can really simulate great teaching, making you think they have what it takes, when they really do not. They seem to show all the special qualities you're looking for during the interview, but when they get into the classroom, all those qualities that you believed they would have, somehow were nowhere to be observed.

When this happens, the key is to recognize where they are lacking, as soon as possible, and jump into action very quickly with support, support, and more support! As leaders, we are tasked with providing teachers with the coaching and accountability they need, in order to be their very best for kids. If support and coaching doesn't work, it's time to start with the black and white—approved prescriptive plans of assistance. This plan helps people recognize their strengths but focus on their weaknesses. They are to review this document at check-in times to ensure that the necessary growth is occurring. Although I really hate placing people on plans or writing them up, sometimes, it's just necessary. At the end of the day, the most important thing is to be able to move the kids from point A to point B. If you're not moving or impacting our kids and you can't be coached into doing so, teaching is not your forte. There are also those "aha" moments when the teachers themselves realize they are not a good fit for the job, even before we are able to recognize it. You'll hear them say things like, "I thought I was going to like teaching, but this is just not for me." They're not even interested in receiving any coaching or support; they just want to break out of there and move on to something else.

One of the things I always emphasized with my staff is that we should never, ever be without someone knowledgeable to instruct the students if a teacher is out, whether that teacher has jumped ship, or if they are simply out sick for some time. We should always have someone waiting in the wings to jump in and take over. In order to make this happen, ensure that you are prepared with knowledgeable instructors in two ways. First, most of my assistant principals are certified in the subject areas they supervise. Thus, if one of the teachers in the area that they supervised was out for any reason, that assistant principal could step in and take over the class, until a certified teacher could be found. Second, we hired content-knowledgeable substitute teachers, which allowed them to jump right in, when need be. If something went wrong with a teacher, we could easily pull a sub from what they were doing, and place them in the class; however, we didn't like having subs teaching a class for an extended amount of time. Our kids must have stability in order to learn, so we do everything we can to put someone in the classroom that is going to stick with them, and we do this as soon as possible. With these systems of classroom coverage in place, the kids can continue learning without missing a beat.

The "Extra" Work of Working at Our School

I understood that teaching at a school like ours and all of the "extra" that's required isn't for everyone. I know this to be a fact, because not all of the new teachers that we hired over the summer stuck with us. Once some of them saw how much work teaching at our school was actually going to entail and all that we required of them, it was too overwhelming. They couldn't cut the mustard, and they knew it. Thus, they decided that it just wasn't for them, and they left right in the middle of the school year. We probably had about three teachers leave the school in the middle of the school year during the time I was principal.

I'm not unrealistic. I know that it takes extra—a lot of extra—to work at a turnaround campus. Everyone must be all in, assuming roles they did not sign up for. All the teachers have to become monitors with assigned days, times, and locations. They also have to participate in data analysis sessions, using data to drive their instruction instead of just going off the cuff in their teaching. Teachers can't just walk into the classroom and begin teaching; they must engage in at-bats—the rehearsal of a lesson in front of peers, receiving feedback, implementing that feedback, then executing with students. This means that they have to prepare early, study their lessons, tweak their lesson (if need be), then teach the lessons again in the classroom. All of that takes extra time, I know. These extra activities might not be required for the average teaching job, but this campus was not your average campus. It takes everything in you, and then some, to help your students succeed.

Believe it or not, most of what it takes to provide the students with the extra they need isn't the extra time involved in the workday; it's the extra *mental energy* that's involved. The job is mentally taxing because there's just so much to get done in one day. There are so many kids who are behind needing to be brought up to grade level proficiencies, and they are counting on you to help them get there. However, as you try to help them get there by teaching them in the classroom, you also have to contend with the types of behavioral issues that are common in schools like ours. Some students' behaviors will keep you from getting through the lesson the way you'd planned. It may also be harder to do small group lessons because they're so active, and also because there's only one of you to monitor 25 of them. In addition to bringing them all the way up to grade level and facilitating the classroom like a pro, you carry the weight of wanting to see them succeed. You put pressure on yourself to ensure the plans are executed, the lessons are taught, and you're doing all you can to help them pass; not letting them down. They need you to give your all—your absolute best every day—regardless of the challenges they put in your way, while you're trying to help them succeed. Taking all of these things on every day, from early in the morning to late in the evening, can definitely take its toll.

A big part of the "extra" is the extra hours our teachers worked on campus. For example, we stayed late – two additional hours – every other Wednesday. We used that time to meet any need that we'd seen as a campus, as well as any area needing support. It consisted of professional learning for English Learners (EL students), professional learning for special education students, social emotional training or data disaggregation.

One session we held was for "extra" teacher development, showing teachers the importance of checking students' understanding by asking questions in the classroom. That came as a result of observations. We would see teachers teaching their hearts out, but never once asking their kids if they understood what was being taught. Then, their kids would bomb their assessments, and the teachers would say, "I taught that so well! It was such a good lesson. I don't understand why the kids didn't do well!" To me, the explanation was a simple one: they never asked the kids any questions the entire time they were teaching. Therefore, even though the kids were sitting there listening to all of the information, the teacher never asked them to repeat it or explain it back in order to know if they were digesting the taught information.

In more advanced academic environments, students are more apt to sit and absorb all the information their teacher gives, 30 minutes straight. Many times, they have been trained to sit still and take notes from the lesson or record the lesson on their phone. They know how to process the information as it's being delivered to them and ask clarifying questions. When they don't want to ask the teacher, they also know how to lean over and ask a friend for clarity when they didn't understand something. Things don't work this way with students who have not experienced that foundation.

Many times students have not been given such tools or developed such listening and comprehension skills over time. For the most part, in the environments in which I've worked for the past 20 years, teachers can't just keep talking to students for 30 minutes and expect them to retain all of the information! Teachers have to break things down, stop and ask questions, and listen to the feedback from students to gauge whether they are actually getting it. In fact, our guideline was that every seven minutes, the teacher had to stop lecturing and check for understanding by asking the appropriate questions. If the information wasn't sticking for students, the teacher had to pivot by changing how the information was being taught. If it's all auditory learning, there might be a switch to visual learning. If it's visual learning, there might be a switch to tactile, hands-on learning. Whatever is needed to keep the kids' attention and help them grasp the concept, this is what teachers must do. When teachers put in the time to do the extra, all these methods and approaches really can get a kid to be on board and engaged.

This is just one example of the type of support and professional development we delivered at our school -making the need to stay late of utmost importance. Teachers had to be able to hone their teaching skills through ongoing coaching, support, and professional development, in order to be their most effective. We put in the extra time doing all of these things to ensure our kids were (and remain) successful.

Most importantly, because the district understood the type of school that we were, and all of the extra work that our teachers had to do, both in and out of the classroom, their compensation was extra—a lot more than they would normally make as a teacher. When they signed on to teach, they got a bonus from a program introduced for struggling campuses in the district. It was a research-based action plan to support, strengthen, and empower underserved and underperforming feeder pattern communities. However, beyond the signing bonus, our teachers and staff were also compensated for their extra time. For example, if we asked them to come in and work Saturday to backwards plan so that they could make sure they're meeting all the demands of the kids, we paid them for that. I wouldn't dare ask my teachers and staff to volunteer their time on a Saturday at work without compensating them. There are some people who might say, "You couldn't pay me enough to work at that school!" I get that. However, I could ensure that the people who worked with me could never say they weren't compensated for the work they were asked to do. They did extra, so they were paid for their time and work. To me, and I'm sure to parents and the district, it was worth every penny.

**

That entire summer after I became principal, my dream team of assistant principals and I did two things: we hired, and we planned. After we hired and planned, we hired and planned again. We repeated this process over and over again. By the end of July, we had succeeded in replacing a large percentage of the teaching staff—a huge challenge completed in record time. We taught all the teachers our standard campus protocols, systems, and expectations, helped them understand the urgency of the situation we were faced with in turning the school around, and readied them for the new school year.

Dr. Campbell is in the business of turning schools around, and… everybody knows that it's a hard job, but what you'll find is that teachers, administrators and anybody will follow her wherever she goes! It's because of who she is as a leader. You have to make sure that the people that work for you feel valued, appreciated, and respected as a human being first before they get into the work. I feel like that's why she's been so successful. She has the type of personality when, if you say we're working until nine or ten o'clock, you don't mind. She's here with you, and you're having fun, so you don't mind doing it. It's a hard job but this is my most favorite job that I've ever had!

– C. Berry, English Teacher

Now that everything was ready and in place for the start of the 2017 - 2018 school year, I could turn my full attention to another urgent matter: having my baby. Although I could have taken a longer leave, I understood that the school district, the community, and everyone who knew anything that was happening with the school would be wondering where I was, how long I would be out, how the school was running without me, and what was going to happen to the school in my absence. Coming off of maternity leave early would ease their concerns and reassure them that I was ready to do the work of turning around the school.

Although I understood their concerns, even with the hurricane, I was settled that everything was fine at the school while I was away. During those five weeks, I was in constant contact with my assistant principals every single day. Working by phone and email, I was making sure that everything we had planned to be done was actually being done, and that everything was running like a well-oiled machine. An outsider looking at my team would have said that they were operating at full speed, executing the plan. However,

I looked at how they operated through the laser-sharp lens of a transformational leader, so I saw lots of coaching and training that still needed to be done. I can still say I am *very* proud of how my team kept things going and how they operated according to the plan while I was away!

One of the things that gave me the greatest sense of confidence while I was out was that I knew I had hired the best teachers for the job, so they wouldn't need me to physically be there providing them with constant support. Most of all, many of my new hires were master teachers with a proven track record of success. My teachers knew that if they'd demonstrated to me how successful they could be, I was hands off, unless they needed me. As long as they were teaching the kids, delivering proven results day in and day out, I'd leave them alone and let them do their thing. There was never a valid reason to go into a teacher's classroom and demand to see all kinds of "fluff" if it wasn't going to have an impact on student growth and understanding. Instead, I kept the focus on the bottom line: simply teach the kids. I got them whatever they needed, from tutors to additional resources, so that they could do the best possible job, which was teaching our kids.

The only exception to that rule was when I had to work with brand new teachers who had never been in the classroom before. For them, I would provide multiple layers of support. In fact, I would tell them up front that I was going to give them the support they needed until they couldn't stand it anymore! Then, once they showed that they didn't need as much support by delivering great results, I'd back up. However, for the initial phase of teaching in the classroom, I would be there every day for them, making sure they had everything they needed to be effective. While I was away, my assistant principals provided this support to the teachers. When I came back to campus, I took the lead on support, because ultimately, their effectiveness was my responsibility.

In addition to hiring the right teachers over the summer, providing them with ongoing support was one of the key success factors that helped us to achieve the levels of success we reached that year. Every one of them will tell you that I considered it my primary job to make sure they always had everything they needed, whether I directly supported them, or appointed one of my hand-picked, highly-qualified assistant principals to do something for them (and I would always go back and ensure that the support I requested for the teacher was delivered). I never sat in my office much, and when I did, I always had an open-door policy; teachers could stop in at any time. I made it a point to stay visible to everyone and walked around. A lot. None of my teachers could ever say, "Oh, I really needed you last week, but I couldn't find you!" I was always available. I did this because I understood the fact that you can't run a school from an office. You've got to be visible and accessible to the people you lead.

I also enforced the same "high visibility" policy with my assistant principals. In the second semester of that year, I had all my assistant principals move their desks out into the hallways, so that the teachers would know they always had access to them. We did not want to give the teachers any excuse for why they were not effective in teaching their kids. With my team members always visible, if a teacher was experiencing an excessively disruptive kid, he or she could open the classroom door, look out into the hallway, and get the immediate support they needed. All the teacher had to say was, "I need this kid out of here. Can you please talk to him? When he's ready to come back to class, he can, but I need someone to deal with him right now." Then, the assistant principal would handle the situation, so the teacher could get back to focusing on instruction.

I ultimately made lots of changes among my assistant principals and my teachers, providing training, support, coaching, and mentorship. I had my dream team of administrative leaders and the top teachers in the profession, and every single day, I invested my time and energy into making them better, so that we could win.

When the school year began, we had one year to ensure that we met performance standards on the STAAR test in order to avoid being shut down. People said it couldn't be done. Everyone bet against us. However, because I had hired, trained, and coached the *right* people, putting them in the right places, our kids performed well on their STAAR tests, and we met TEA performance standards. In fact, not only did we accomplish this great feat in only one year, we also got our early college designation, which allowed us to have our kids take college courses while they attended their classes on our school's campus, meaning they could earn an associate's degree at the same time they graduated with their high school diploma! Together, we turned around the campus. Our story goes to show the importance of a great team when approaching a turnaround challenge!

Mastering Motivation, Morale, and Inspiration with Teachers

Once we hit the ground running for the fall 2017 semester, we had our challenges with teachers. This was to be expected; it's something with which every leadership team at every school has to deal with. The two main areas I dealt with among my teachers were motivating them to maintain their belief in the kids' abilities to learn and maintaining their composure in the classroom.

The most common motivational conversation I had with my teachers was about the need for them to remain committed to the belief that our kids could (and can) do anything. Despite how far behind the kids were, despite their discipline issues, and even despite the kids fighting against their teachers' efforts to bring them up to grade level standards, teachers must never lose sight of the fact that our kids were *(and are)* capable of learning! In fact, kids are *more* than capable. Teachers can never allow the challenges and obstacles they face in the classroom to make them abandon all hope that the kids can learn.

The second most common motivational conversation that I had with my teachers was about maintaining their composure in the classroom. At every turnaround school I've ever led, I've always been up front with my teachers that they would be dealing with classroom discipline issues at another level. This was also true at our school. Whether intentionally or unintentionally, kids are notorious for pushing teachers' buttons, activating their triggers, and doing whatever is necessary to frustrate them, causing them to become bothered and off task. Kids are masters at it! However, even when the classroom is going crazy, teachers cannot lose their composure and speak to the kids unprofessionally. If they do, they especially shouldn't be surprised when kids respond. Instead of blowing their cool or losing their composure, we coached our teachers with different methods of response. The end result was taking a deep breath, reminding themselves that their students were still children, and responding in a professional, calm, civil, and respectful manner.

Don't get me wrong. It's not that we allowed the kids to have the run of the campus, doing whatever they wanted, provoking the teachers, and getting away with it because we protected them from any consequences. We were very supportive of our teachers when they were dealing with discipline issues in the classroom. For example, if a student was becoming too disruptive, or was being disrespectful to the teacher, we would remove the kid from the classroom. Sometimes, we would take them out for a cooling off period, and other times, we placed them in in-school suspension— whatever was commensurate with their behavior issue. Knowing that they were fully supported by the staff and administrators was motivation in and of itself. On the other hand, we trained our teachers in Social Emotional Learning so that situations that escalated in prior years would not continue. The response that teachers gave to misbehavior was the game changer.

Outside of the classroom, my team and I always tried to do things that kept the teachers just as excited about coming to school as we did for the kids. Thus, in addition to encouraging and motivating our teachers, my team and I were also intentional about doing little things that boosted morale and inspired them. We treated our teaching staff extremely well, and we fed them whenever possible. For example, when I first got to the high school, we only had one lunch period during which all of the students ate together. This meant that we could have administrators on duty to monitor lunch, and all the teachers were off at the same time. At least once a month, we would throw a "Party With a Purpose," just for the teachers and students. We provided a DJ and other amenities needed to put on a really fun lunchtime party. If the month had a prominent theme, like Valentine's Day, we would celebrate that day during the party. During the week of spring break, we would have the party at the end of the week, leading into the vacation, as a send-off for our teachers. Besides curriculum, that was my favorite part! We engaged everyone in the community we could find to sponsor teacher lunches, donate gift cards, and we had two staff members that were resident DJs, and loved to jam!

Testing was also a great time for us to celebrate our teachers. Before the STAAR testing week began, we would do just that; celebrate! On testing day, we provided food for our teachers before, during, and even after testing as treats, so they wouldn't have to leave campus at all. Even though we did this to show our appreciation for the hard work they'd invested in getting our students prepared for the assessments, it was also a win for us: it ensured that we didn't have to worry about them leaving campus to go eat, potentially returning late, delaying the start of their next round of testing. The same was true for training and professional development days.

Fortunately, we've developed some strong relationships with community partners, who were always willing to provide food when the time came to celebrate and appreciate our teachers. For example, when we wanted Tex-Mex food, Gringos, a local Houston favorite, would sponsor the food for us. Sometimes, the food we purchased for our teachers would be as simple as boudin-on-a-stick, which was a treat that our teachers loved. Other times, we would have a full meal; a three-course spread. For breakfast, we would have a breakfast bar, complete with cereal, milk, donuts, breakfast tacos, and all the fixings. This was super cost-effective, and we all pitched in to purchase one thing. Other times, my secretary, who was an avid coupon clipper, would find sodas on sale, and buy a few cases, along with single serve bags of chips. We'd all split the cost and pay pennies on the dollar. We would simply run into each teacher's classroom with a surprise snack, like chips and a soda, with a cute note attached. As we delivered them, I would have the kids in the class cheer for their teachers, because these men and women didn't *have* to do the great job they were doing to teach their students.

Aside from food, our community partners were always willing to offer lots of other perks. For example, they might give us tickets for our teachers to experience certain events like the Houston Rodeo (a *really* big event in Houston!), concerts, plays, etc. We would give these perks to our teachers to celebrate them for things like best attendance, having all their non-negotiables done, and any other reason we could find to celebrate them, making them feel appreciated.

Most of all, we kept our teachers motivated, and the morale high by keeping things fun. With everything we did, from trainings, to meetings, and everything in-between, we tried to foster a lively, fun atmosphere. While the food helped, there were other factors that went into ensuring campus efficacy. For instance, we worked in teams a lot. Anytime we did activities, we tried to always do them as a team, because collaborating with others tends to be a lot more fun than doing things in isolation. Things like this kept our atmosphere from being dry and humdrum when we got together, and they helped teachers enjoy their teaching experiences at our school.

I should note that when I say teachers enjoyed teaching at our school, this is not something based on speculation; it's based on the numbers. You see, in a neighborhood like ours, it's difficult to keep teachers on a school campus. In fact, most all school campuses that look like ours typically have a tremendous number of vacancies, because teachers don't want to work in such difficult settings. Nevertheless, not only did we not have any vacancies, but in the 2018-2019 year, we didn't have a single teacher leave our campus, unless it was due to a promotion. In the previous school year, we had the three at Christmas, but after that only one or two left at the end of the school year, which, relative to other campuses, was a phenomenal retention rate. The fact that teachers chose to remain at the high school, an admittedly difficult campus to teach at, spoke volumes about the support they received. That support went beyond their particular academic course, allowing us to provide them with any support they needed for classroom management.

Chapter 4
Transformational Leadership Tips

TLT 4.1
Hiring Challenge 1: Inviting Star
Assistant Principals to Win

- Identify what skill(s) your APs can bring, and allow them to coach each other up.

- Create a coaching plan that details who's responsible for what. Assign tasks to your team.

- Properly identify roles of administrators so that they are utilized at maximum capacity.

- Identify specific trainings for your team. Once the trainings are identified and completed, begin discussing what implementation will look like. Delegate APs to carry out the implementation.

- Include your admin on the creation of goals (weekly, bi-weekly, end of grading cycle, semester, and yearly goals). The goals should be visible and discussed on a regular basis via individual and whole-group check-ins.

TLT 4.2
Hiring Challenge 2: Identifying Coachable,
Qualified Teachers

- Exhibit transparency during interviews. This will save time and energy in the long haul, preventing a principal from having to rehire in the middle of the year due to a teacher quitting.

- Be willing to pay for what you expect from your teachers.

TLT 4.3
Hiring Challenge 3: Getting the Right Teachers with the Right Fit in the Right Places

- Understand the importance of outlining success factors when selecting candidates, and what those factors look like. Be sure to determine what types of questions should be asked in advance.

- Create an action plan of support for a teacher at the very first sign of a problem arising.

- Outline a system for classroom coverage, having at least two options.

TLT 4.4
Success Factor 1: Do They Know Their Stuff?

- Hire candidates who possess relationship-building skills and content knowledge. These two critical keys are essential when constructing relationships and building capacity within kids.

- It's key to ask tons of questions so that you will understand the candidate's stance and whether they are the right fit for your campus and its needs.

- When you hire smart and unpack who the candidate is by discovering their skills and personality, they have a higher likelihood of adding value to the team and the vision.

TLT 4.5
Success Factor 2: Can They Relate to the Kids?

- Regardless of how trained, skilled or talented a teacher is, without the ability to relate with the kids, they will not be successful in a turnaround environment. Listen beyond their words as you interview them to be able to discern whether their personality is a match for being able to connect with the kids in the school.

TLT 4.6
Success Factor 3: Are They Willing to Go the Extra Mile?

- Teachers must possess empathy towards kids while also pushing them towards academic success. Consider having a pre-service training grounded in SEL (Social Emotional Learning) so that the entire building is well versed in what it takes to go the extra mile.

TLT 4.7
Success Factor 4: Are They Coachable?

- Assess the candidate's level of coachability by asking the following questions:

  - When is the last time you failed?
  - Who coached you through success after that failure?
  - What did those success steps look like?

- When coaching teachers up, ponder the following:
  - How to plan for kids who are academically lower than expected.
  - How to design a plan for kids who are more academically advanced, including differentiating the learning to keep them engaged and ahead.

- How to strategize a plan of action for excessively disruptive students, including having expectations, rules, consequences and a rewards system (which will incentivize kids) in place.

TLT 4.8
The "Extra" Work of Working in a Turnaround School

• Expect teachers to embed checks for understanding (CFUs) in the lesson plan, during at-bats and live lessons. Don't be afraid to have your teachers put in the extra work to see results. This creates buy-in from students.

• Be visible and accessible always.

TLT 4.9
Mastering Motivation, Morale, and Inspiration with Teachers

• Coach teachers on the correct way to respond to misbehavior. Consider having your entire staff trained in Social Emotional Learning. This can serve as a game changer, equipping teachers with the needed tools to respond correctly to students.

• Identify multiple morale boosters and use them often!

5

From Stranger to Superhero: Educator Saves the Day

Winning Over Sunnyside & the Houston Community

"Who is *she*? She's not from this community! We didn't even interview her! How is *she* the new principal?" These were only *some* of the sentiments of the highly irritated community members that sat before me the day I was being introduced as the new principal of the high school. There I was, sitting in the school library in my flowered shirt, business suit, and signature high heels, looking professional and composed on the outside, but priming myself for this strenuous meeting. I did my best to prevent my facial expression from communicating to the unreceptive crowd how I felt about going into the situation, but I felt *confidently* uncertain.

With every question and concern that was explicitly voiced, there were so many more that were implied or suggested, each pointing to why I should not have been selected as the high school's new principal. For example, there was the glaring fact that I was a female. If it were up to the community, they would have preferred a strong, black male come in and take over the school.

Next, there was the issue of the community's choice of principal versus the school district's choice of principal. Typically, the community would have a voice and play a significant role in selecting the leader. There would have been a formal hiring process, complete with an interview panel, input from community members, etc. However, at the time I was selected as principal, the school was in a very tumultuous situation. As a turnaround campus in need of a drastic transformation in record time, unprecedented measures were taken. Under serious, time-sensitive conditions like these, the school district has the right to bypass all of the formalities of the hiring process, including the community's input, and put someone whom they deem to be the best candidate in place as principal. This is exactly what the district had done, and some of the community didn't like it. Thus, on the day that I was presented as the new principal of the high school, I faced a somewhat hostile crowd.

As soon as the representative from the school district opened the community meeting by welcoming the crowd, introduced me, and explained the purpose of the gathering, the flood gates opened with question, after question, after question. "Is she from our community?" someone asked. Another person stood up and immediately answered that I wasn't, and that I was actually from the north side of Houston. "How can she lead a school in this community and not even know the community?" another person asked with concern. Finally, I interrupted and interjected, "I was born and raised 12 minutes away from this high school, and I am very familiar with the area." Although that had been a concern, once it was no longer valid, the subject changed, but the questions were just as spirited. Questions regarding everything under the sun began flying. What is her track record? What schools has she turned around before? How was she chosen? Who interviewed her? Why was she a candidate for the job? Being principal of this school is a step down from her previous job as a school support officer in the district. Why would she take a demotion? Did you put her in our school because she wasn't doing a good job where she was? Did you give us a failing administrator because our school is already failing? What makes her think she can turn this high school around? Are the teachers here going to be fired? How many teachers did she get rid of at the previous schools you said she turned around? There were so many questions. Even my board member (and we still laugh about this today) wanted my bio! She was not afraid to let anyone know that she had her eye on me, too. She wasn't yet convinced of my skills. She, too, wanted what was best for the community she served, as this is what she had been elected to do.

I patiently and assuredly answered all the questions community members had, with the district representative chiming in to add support and validation to what I was saying along the way. I explained that yes, I worked on the north side of Houston. But for those many years of working on the north side, I committed to making a three-hour round-trip commute every day. I also informed them that I had, in fact, worked on the south side, only seven minutes down the road from the high school as a middle school principal for five years. Houston was vast, and if you weren't in this particular high school's feeder pattern, the community had no knowledge of you. I explained my track record of success and how I was committed to achieving the same results at this school, because I believed that the kids deserved more, regardless of the community in which they lived. I made an argument that I had the training, tools, and experience to get the task done, and not only was I qualified for the job, but I had the heart that was necessary to get this win for the school. As they sat and listened to me share my position, my brothers, my husband, and my mother quietly watched the people pulling out their mobile phones, conducting

Google searches on my name to figure out who I was. My family members also heard several of the comments, which we later spoke about at home.

I didn't take the hostile atmosphere of the community meeting personally; I knew their anger wasn't directed toward me. There were a lot more issues they were discontent about, other than the selection of me as the new principal. For example, taxpayers had passed an $80 million bond for the rebuilding of the high schools more than five years prior, and the rebuilding had not been completed. In their eyes, the other schools that were a part of this bond were complete. Why was this the only school that hadn't been completed? They also wanted to talk about the fact that there had been a different principal at the school every other year for the past six years. Why was the turnover so high? They wanted answers to why the school had been failing for nearly 10 years. Why wouldn't the district step in and do something to help them? They wanted answers. They *deserved* answers.

These concerned members of the community were just collectively displeased with the way the school had been handled for so many years. They felt devalued, ignored, and disregarded, like someone was making decisions for them, not with them. For more than 10 years, their school had always been on the losing end of these decisions, and although they asked a lot of questions about these serious matters, they felt they didn't get a lot of answers. The answers that they did receive, they perceived to be "brush off" answers that were meant to silence their concerns for the time being, while nothing ever changed. They had grown skeptical, and rightfully so. I understood this, and I empathized with them. As I listened to their concerns, I anxiously awaited the opportunity to demonstrate to them that I had the plan for what they had been wanting to see happen at the high school all along.

The district representatives tried their best to protect me from the questions hurled at me by community members, because I had just walked in the door; I hadn't even had a chance to get my feet wet yet. However, the community saw things differently. They saw things as, "You're the principal of the school *now*, so you're the one responsible for giving us answers about our school — *right now!* Tell us what we want to know!" I could tell by their conversations that the fundamental question they all had in mind was, "As the new leader of this school, what are you going to do to change what no one else has been able to change?" The reality is that I could have talked all day about what I was planning to do to transform the school and make it successful. However, at the end of the day, it would all have been for naught. No amount of talking would be able to convince a community that I had what it took to undertake the turnaround process. Because of this, I didn't take a lot of time trying to explain; I could show them better than I could tell them. I simply took my last statement as another opportunity to assure them that the district had made the best decision for the school by making me the new principal, and that my goal was to make the school better for the kids and the community.

Yet and still, I also took their skepticism and each one of their concerns, embracing them as a challenge. I absorbed everything they said, making a mental checklist of the things they wanted to see done. I thought to myself, *How many of these things can I check off during my first year as principal?* I was determined to ensure that they received everything on this list, because as concerned members of the community, they deserved both answers and results. It was time to strategically approach winning over this community because my success as a principal depended on it.

Choosing Which Community to Engage to Gain Support for the School's Success

Transformational leaders recognize that they cannot achieve change in any organization by working in a silo. Every organization is surrounded by an external community of players that contribute to its internal success. This means that the engagement of the community must be a critical objective on the action list of any transformational leader.

There are two types of people in the community: (1) those who are vested in the organization's success and (2) those who are not.

Those who are vested might include, for example, people who attended the meeting at which I was introduced as the new principal. They are connected to the organization and have some interest or stake in its success. These are the people who ask questions, read the reports, monitor performance, and expect a certain level of accountability from the leader. They can have either direct or indirect interests in the organization. For instance, the concerned members of the community who have children attending the school have direct interests in the success of the school, while those who don't have children attending the school have indirect interests in the success of the school; concerned citizens with indirect interests might be alumni, members of the community who attended the school but dropped out, or even people who have moved into the community and recognize how important of an institution it is. Whether they have direct or indirect interests in the organization, each of these individuals is vested in the organization's success; having a deep sense that their lives are impacted in some way by the organization's performance.

Then, there are those in the community who are not vested in the organization. These are sometimes businesses, religious or other non-profit organizations, and individuals who live in the community but who do not feel any real connection to it. In our school's case, there were not many who were not vested in some way. Either their family member, friend or pastor – someone they knew closely – had attended the school. But there *were* people who don't have any children attending the school, who don't show up for the meetings, and who have no real interest in staying up to date with what's happening at the school, because they don't feel that it really has an impact on their lives.

I mention these two types of people in the community (those who are vested and those who are not) because engaging both groups should be on the radar of the transformational leader. Some leaders will tend to engage only those who are the active, vocal participants in the community. The leader tries to keep these members satisfied and content with the performance of the organization, so he or she can do his job at hand. In exchange for the satisfactory performance of the leader, some of the members of this community will contribute support as needed. However, they are not the only ones that can provide support; those who are not directly vested in the school can be utilized as support systems to contribute to the school's success. For example, this might include reaching out to professional organizations and corporations in the community, asking them to send mentors to the school to provide guidance and support for the kids. It might mean reaching out to politicians and asking them to make something happen for the kids at our school that we can't make happen for them. There is a plethora of resources in the community without direct interests in the school which can be engaged to help the school succeed. Learning how to engage both those in the community with and without direct interests in the school was a key part of my strategy the support it needed for the turnaround.

Strategic Community Engagement Key 1: Identify & Influence the Key Influencers

Although no one at the initial community meeting had seemed particularly satisfied with the district's selection of their new principal, there was one *exceptionally* vocal community member who wanted to make his dissatisfaction with the process crystal clear. About 30 minutes before the meeting began, this gentleman came to me and said, "Look. Someone whom I like very much speaks highly of you, and that's good. But basically, you're going to have to earn my trust."

I said, "Okay. Who are you? Do you have kids at this campus?"

He replied, "I don't have kids on this campus. Just think of me as someone who has kids everywhere, because I fight for injustices anywhere kids are involved. I can be your worst nightmare."

Undaunted by his threat, I said, "Okay. Well, you don't have to worry about that here, because I'm going to do exactly what I said I will. I'm going to make sure the kids get what they need."

We talked for about 10 minutes. He explained to me that he was going to continue to check up on what was going on in the community, that he had eyes and ears at the school, and he was going to be sure that what I said I was going to do in this meeting, was actually going to happen, and so on. After our exchange, the meeting began.

I know how important it is to have the community on your side as the leader of a school, especially a school that is the focal point of the community. I also know that in every community, you have people who have a significant voice. They use their voices to influence the attitudes and perceptions of the community, and in turn, the community respects and listens to them. This guy was one of those voices, one of those big community influencers. However, I didn't fear him; I just knew that he would hold me accountable for what I said I was going to do. Doing the work that I had promised would be my first assignment in fostering community relations as the new principal of the school.

As time passed, more and more community members became fully engaged. None of the promises that I'd made went unfulfilled, and this was all that was needed to not only receive support, but to become one of the school's biggest advocates in the community.

Strategic Community Engagement Key 2: Communicate Openly and Often

One of the biggest frustrations that the members of the community had concerning the high school in the past was communication: they didn't feel that anyone ever listened to them, and they didn't feel anyone ever told them anything. As a result, they walked around with a lot of questions and no answers. The fact that they were taxpaying citizens who were paying the salaries of people who were supposed to be accountable to them, who were supposed to listen to and respond to them, and yet they were not receiving any communication, disturbed them. It also fostered a high level of distrust. After all, why would the district and school leadership not be totally transparent with them by providing answers to what seemed to be simple, straightforward questions? Were they trying to hide something? Undoubtedly, they felt that their community in which the school was situated had a lot to do with it; people in lower socio-economic communities often grow accustomed to having their concerns re-categorized as complaints and disregarded rather than addressed. Understanding that all everyone really wanted was to be heard and responded to, I made it a part of my community engagement strategy to simply communicate openly and often.

Communication is a two-way street. It's not just about speaking; it's about speaking *and* listening. Therefore, I ensured that I offered opportunities for the people to speak and for me and my team to listen. When I ran into people who had questions, I would hand them my business card and say, "Look, call me this evening or email me all of your questions. I'll answer them at the community meeting." Then, I made sure my staff and I came to the meetings prepared to answer all of the questions with transparency and clarity. We brought along documentation that we could refer to in order to find answers that we didn't have already. At the community meetings, members of the community could ask all of the questions they wanted. If a question was asked that we couldn't find an answer to on the spot, I promised the people that I would find the answer and communicate it to them after the meeting, which I always did. These open public forums offered the best approach to be able to hear and respond to as many people as possible in the same setting; I couldn't be in meetings all day and run a school simultaneously. The people ultimately wanted a better school, and I couldn't give them a better school if I was always in meetings with the community. My first priority was getting kids to succeed in the classroom, thus organizing evening and weekend events that facilitated this type of collective communication was the most efficient, effective approach.

Of course, a vital part of our communication is both sharing information with and listening to the parents. In fact, I always reminded my assistant principals that the majority of their time is going to be communication, whether with students, teachers, or parents. The parental communications always seem to be the most challenging. While we planned organized opportunities to facilitate this communication, like parent-teacher conferences, report card night, etc., some of our parents tended to want to have a different kind of conversation. Some were inclined to be a lot more concerned about their kid's cell phone being taken away. Often, they deemed their child received too harsh a consequence for their violation of a particular rule. For example, if you were on the phone during class, we needed you to stay after school to make up the missed worked. Once we finished explaining the rationale for our rules, most parents understood and actually became our advocates. Thus, we kept the lines of communication fluid with them, invited them to talk about whatever they needed to with us — even if it didn't pertain to academics. Because of my time limitations, I always asked my assistant principals to handle issues initially. If my assistant principal couldn't resolve the issue, or the parent demanded to speak to the principal, I'd always make myself available.

Further, there are rules of engagement that I train my team members to abide by when communicating with parents, students, and community members, especially disgruntled ones. Always give them the benefit of the doubt from the very beginning, even when their stories and explanations seem entirely far-fetched, and somewhat unbelievable. Most importantly, communication should be conducted in such a way that my team members handle people the same way we would want someone to handle our mother, father, or kids. We always err on the side of empathy as we communicate, then we try to provide whatever support we can. Were all calls pleasant? I would be lying if I said they were. What I didn't allow was anyone to disrespect my staff. As long as we were all being respectful, the conversation could last forever, but the minute someone called my staff out of their name or began becoming aggressive, the conversation was over. They could return once they calmed down.

One of my greatest efforts as a leader was making an intentional effort to keep key people in the community informed about what was going on at the school. Even if they didn't ask, I made sure to be proactive in reaching out to them so I could keep them informed about our progress. We were doing some tremendous things at the school, and the community needed to know! They also needed to know what challenges we faced, and what opportunities were available for them to help us get some things done. When possible, I met with anyone who had any kind of stake, interest, or association with the school so that we could determine what role they could play in contributing to the school's success.

For instance, I met with Judge Brown who was over our precinct, and we discussed plans to help our students who had excessive absences attend school. I met with faculty and staff members from Houston Community College because they were our partners for our CTE and college courses. I met with our Houston City Councilman, as well as with the County Commissioner Rodney Ellis, who graciously gave us $10,000 at the beginning of the school year. I even met with our state senator Borris Miles whose mother was a former school Queen on our campus, so he was especially vested in our school. He was the impetus for our Miles Ahead program, a program that invested monies into our campus for black and Hispanic males so we could support them, catapulting them to success!

One of our biggest ways to communicate was the "Southside Take Over Parade," which we birthed and hosted for the past few years at the beginning of every school year. We had all of the high-powered political officials at the parade, from Mayor Sylvester Turner to County Commissioner Rodney Ellis, to State Senator Borris Miles, to Representative Shawn Thierry, Jackie Robinson (the alumni association president), Judson Robinson and John Robinson from the Houston Area Urban League, local elementary and middle schools, and anyone else in the community who had any role in influencing our community in a positive way. We also had the "Mayor of Sunnyside," Sandra Hines, who had been invested in our community for years! We gathered all of these people together, got the city to shut down a few streets in the neighborhood, and hosted a grand parade! My vision for establishing this parade was to feature everything about the southside that was good.

Everything from floats to decorated cars, the Corvette Club, to different community organizations participating, to the live music of marching bands, all made the event one for the books. I mention this parade not because it had anything directly to do with the school's academics, but it gave the community the opportunity to see all that we had in place to help not only our students but the entire community. We facilitated giving away uniforms and school supplies, had hearing tests done, eye exams, tested community members for diabetes, introduced them to our campus Baylor College Clinic, and had local businesses advertise and sell their products. The campuses that fed into us were pivotal in the parade's success. Area principals were invested, from bringing volunteers to showcasing their baby marching bands! We always had more than 2,000 people in attendance. All of our key players committed to the success of the parade, and the icing on the cake was the "movers and shakers" saw firsthand our commitment to students and all that we had to celebrate—they pledged their support for our school. And because they saw the commitment that my team and I had for students and the community, I was able to stay in constant personal communication with them. In fact, anytime we had an event at school, we invited them all to come to our school to experience it with us. As a result, to this day, they are vested in the high school in ways they previously were not. Now, they would come to me and ask, "Hey, how are you doing? How can we help you?" They provided us with everything from gift cards, to snacks for our snack store, to scholarships for our students, and more – all for the kids.

Our high school's alumni were strong and amazing. Jackie Johnson (the president of one of the chapters) and I stay in constant contact with each other. This group not only gave consistent scholarships, but they also supported monetarily throughout the year, and in person, whenever necessary. And to think, all of that happened because of intentional communication with key influencers in the community.

My team and I were extremely intentional about representing our high school at meetings hosted by other individuals and organizations in the community. Our presence at those meetings helped the community to see that we were interested and vested in what was going on in the Sunnyside community. Most importantly, it helped to develop relationships with them, raising our level of trustworthiness and credibility. We gave up many evenings and weekends to attend community meetings at the local church in the community, community centers, and any other place where meetings were being held to discuss topics like what could be done to combat violence in the community, how to get community members more involved in bettering the community, and the like. Although these meetings were not directly about our school, each of them had a direct effect on our school, because the outcomes affected our kids. Remember: communication is not always about speaking; it's about listening to what others have to say and staying informed. Principals, especially those who serve in communities like the one surrounding our school, have to keep their finger on the pulse of what's happening in the community. It takes time, but it's necessary.

Strategic Community Engagement Step 3: Get the Community (Resources) Into the School and the School Into the Community

Maintaining communication with individuals and organizations outside of the school is a huge part of being a successful administrator. There are so many resources in the community that a school like ours could leverage for its success, and I set out to identify and engage as many of them as possible. Our high school is not like schools in more affluent school districts that have immediate access to lots of resources. When working in a school in a less privileged area, it is the work of the leader to come up with creative ways to "find" the resources necessary to help the kids succeed. Yes, we did the traditional fundraisers to try to generate funds for the things that our kids wanted and needed that weren't funded by the school district. However, even with fundraisers, we fell significantly short of the resources that we needed to make our students successful. Where resources are lacking, creativity and out-of-the-box thinking must abound!

To creatively compensate for our school's lack of access to resources, we made it a part of our engagement plan to get the community—and its resources—into the school, and to get the school's students into the community to take advantage of the resources it had to offer. One thing that I always told my staff was, "I don't care what you have to do. Call and ask for what we need, because a closed mouth doesn't get fed!" We could talk all day about what resources we didn't have and what people wouldn't do for our students, but until we actually asked, we'd have no idea whether they would give us access to the resources they had. It never hurts to ask!

For example, we would call companies and ask them for the opportunity to allow our kids to come to their sites for a career field trip without charging us anything. We also asked for tours, and to have some of their leaders and employees talk to our kids in order to expose them to different career options. Then, on top of that, we would ask them to provide lunch for our kids while they were there, because we didn't have additional funding to purchase food. We made some bold requests! Sometimes, there were "No's," but you'd be surprised at how many people responded to our requests with "Yes!" Occasionally, the company would say "Yes" to us coming to visit, but they wouldn't agree to purchase the food. However, instead of letting the kids miss out on the opportunity, our school cafeteria would provide sack lunches, so they could still attend. Depending on the company we visited, it was required that our students be professionally dressed. Most of our kids didn't have anything that would be considered professional attire in their wardrobe. What did staff like Ms. Jolivet and Ms. Charles and Ms. Walker do? They went into their own pockets to buy the kids what they needed, so they could get the exposure. Or we'd have people who donated several sets of professional pants and shirts. They went to places like Goodwill and bought jackets, pants, dresses, and whatever else our kids needed, so they could look professional during their career outings, getting our school out into the community to take advantage of those resources.

I also did everything possible to get the community and its resources into our school. I had dreamed of having a mentorship program for our campus since my first year, but it was a *huge* undertaking! I pitched the idea to some up-and-coming teachers on campus, and they were all in! It just so happened that because of one of our community partners, Mrs. Marten, we had developed a relationship with Michael Berry (from the nationally-syndicated *Michael Berry Show*). He advertised on his show our need for mentors, and Mrs. Watson, Mr. Riley, Mr. Edwards, Ms. Johnson, Ms. Cook, Mr. Tigner, Ms. Villareal, and Mrs. Barrera started to develop our kick-off. I called upon our Commissioner, Rodney Ellis, who secured the Buffalo Soldier Museum for us, we got a DJ, Roger Ybarra (owner of Gringo's Mexican Grill) donated the food for the two-day event (one for the boys and one for the girls), we made balloon arches, Ms. Jefferson made pink lemonade for the girls and a Sprite deluxe for the boys, and it turned out to be one of the most memorable events of my principalship. It's hard to frame in words, but that day, there was a spirit in the air, and everyone felt it. I took my team to dinner afterwards. They had worked really hard to make that day happen, and it was absolutely worth it! We approached some of the top corporations and organizations in the greater Houston community to recruit some high-powered men and women to come in and mentor our kids. Those mentors from the community were asked to have lunch with our students once a month, and to initiate conversations throughout the month with them.

Another way that we got the community into our school was through the donation of things that the school couldn't afford to provide the students. One of the most common donations we saw from the community was restaurant donations. Rewarding our kids for their hard work was one of our campus values, and our kids always loved receiving these types of rewards. You would think that kids would ask for a variety of different things as rewards, but usually they didn't. We always tried to make that request a reality. We petitioned a lot of local companies to donate items when it was time to reward the kids. If they weren't able to donate 100% of the request, we asked them to at least go half with us and then we'd ask alumni or one of our other partners to take care of the other half. We successfully formed relationships with Gringo's owner Russell Ybarra and with Ms. Etta's Catering, so we always knew where we could turn for a celebration! If you use food as a reward, keep in mind to always follow mandated food guidelines, both district and federal.

We met Mr. Ybarra through Ms. Martens, who you'll learn of shortly, from Lighthouse. I remember when Mr. Ybarra came to the school to speak to the kids about doing well, entrepreneurship, and being good individuals. He handed each one of them a red envelope. He explained to them that one of the envelopes had a 100 dollar bill in it and that whoever received it must pay some of it forward! Everyone in the room agreed to do so. They were super excited about seeing who the lucky winner was. When Mr. Ybarra said, "You may now open your envelope!" the kids went crazy! He had given each child a crisp, new 100 dollar bill. The kids were elated and talked about this event for weeks. What makes you pause, though, is that these kids were so amazing that although they were not wealthy by any measure, they still shared with the less fortunate in their paying it forward promise – and they were proud to do so.

There were individuals out there with the power to singlehandedly transform huge parts of our campus! Some are aforementioned, and others, like Ms. Martens and Ms. Gambrell, were mainstays for years on our campus. When I first started at the school, there were two important groups in operation. One was the Lighthouse for Students, founded and run by Ms. Kelly Martens. The other was No More Victims, founded and run by Ms. Marilyn Gambrell.

Lighthouse was created after Ms. Kelly Martens ran across an article about the campus. Her exact words were, "God led me here to do this work." She brought in guest speakers and food, held events to raise money, took kids in need to camp, and introduced the kids to influential people who would go on to help them in life. Because of her, the students were even able to meet Beyoncé through their healing work with Hurricane Harvey! Most importantly, Ms. Martens was committed. Her visits were weekly and on time. She and a crew of people she assembled, both men and women, worked together to support the school under her leadership. She was a white woman who drove 35 miles one way not to "save" but to "serve" the students of Sunnyside. I was thankful for her.

Bless our Dr. Campbell-Rhone. Working with her over the past three years has been a wonderful experience. She was a brilliant principal that came into the high school having so many challenges. Dr. Campbell-Rhone shared with all of us her tremendous compassion, leadership skills and commitment, not only to her students, but to her staff, organizations on campus and the Sunnyside community. Dr. Campbell-Rhone was such a pleasure to work with. Under her leadership, the high school evolved from being on the verge of closing to a powerful and successful high school. We are so fortunate to have her, not only in the district and Houston, Texas, but as a true leader for our children in this country. Her in-depth understanding of the needs of the students and her commitment to addressing those needs have tremendously impacted and empowered their lives. Dr. Campbell-Rhone is legendary. She has greatly enriched the lives of our No More Victims Family and we are deeply grateful for her. I will always consider Dr. Campbell-Rhone a dear friend!

– Marilyn Gambrell, No More Victims

Ms. Marilyn Gambrell, known widely as "Momma G," decided years ago that she would dedicate her life to helping students of incarcerated or murdered parents. The things she has done for kids will amaze you. Kids call her at two o'clock in the morning, and she is available. A very tender-hearted but tough woman, she takes on the spirit of the students, carries their burdens, and ensures they have the proper counseling, nourishment, and supplies necessary to thrive. She was there to assist with and celebrate alongside any "win" for our school and to cry for any travesty – and we had those (far too many to count).

One of the young men named Devon, who participated in No More Victims when he was younger, grew up to become one of the program's biggest advocates. While working with the program and mentoring kids at the school, he was simultaneously working to receive his doctorate from Columbia University. I remember when he interviewed me about my perception of No More Victims in school and the importance of the outlet for students. He was impressively intelligent. Soon thereafter, Devon was murdered. It was a huge blow for Momma G, me, and the program. And to think, soon after that, we were consoling students whose parents were murdered in front of them or sentenced to years in the penitentiary. The stories would blow your mind. Momma G was needed. She has and will always have my utmost respect.

I am a firm believer that what you put out returns to you ten-fold, and that was true throughout my time as principal of the school. Several angels, including Julian Rhyne, appeared to bless our campus with so many "wins." We were fortunate enough to garner our girls a visit with my Forever First Lady, Michelle Obama. Julian supported special events where we invited all of the feeder pattern schools to our campus for a Winter Wonderland, where they received free toys and gifts. This was not only good for our kids to participate in giving back, but it was also good for the younger students to see how the campus had changed and become excited about what was happening in that building. When we took the kids on a college trip, Julian helped us get a tour of the U.S. Capitol Building and made sure that we met Robin Roberts on the morning show *Good Morning America*. He provided snacks and drinks for different events and was a comedian to boot! His ingredients made everything better. One of our local barbers, Joseph Rockamore, better known as "Rock," partnered with us to wash, braid, and cut more than 500 heads in one day on the Saturday before school began. We had backpacks, school supplies, music, and giveaways for all of the neighborhood!

We had a local news reporter, Jonathon Martin, visit our campus, bringing a star-studded panel to candidly speak to students about going *Beyond The Game*, which inspired young men to dream big beyond sports. These panels included former NFL player LeMarcus Newman, Ralph Sampson III, and Mathew Knowles, amongst other well-known celebrities that the boys were familiar with or loved. National rap artists Lil' Flip and Lil' Keke, both alumni of our school, represented their community with appearances and scholarships for our students, and we even had school alumnus and Hall of Fame football player Mike Singletary grace our students with encouraging words as we were named a Hall of Fame High School because of his athletic acumen. State Senator Borris Miles selected our campus to be a part of his "Miles Ahead" initiative, a group for young men of color that mentors and monitors a select group of students to ensure they are college bound!

So many people played integral roles in the life of our school that I can't name them all. If I failed to mention anyone, charge it to my head and not my heart. We are forever grateful for anyone who invested in our school and the Sunnyside community.

> In the 2016-2017 school year, Campbell-Rhone was named a School Support Officer for the same district she previously attended, taught, and led. When asked to support [the] High School, she noticed that some of her former students were not performing to their fullest potential. As a result, when the principal position became available, she was determined to commit to helping [it to] become a successful school once more.
>
> – *African American News and Issues*, March 11, 2019

Chapter 5
Transformational Leadership Tips

TLT 5.1
Get to Know Your Community

- Hear their concerns. Also, create a checks and balances system to ensure their requests are noted and that every effort is made to resolve those concerns.

- Allow the community to aid in the creation of transformational change. Without them, you will not successfully thrive.

- Get all community members, large and small, vested in the school and its mission and vision.

TLT 5.2
Strategic Community Engagement Key 1:
Identify & Influence the Key Influencers

- Communicate openly and often with community stakeholders. Not only will you have to speak, but you must genuinely listen.

TLT 5.3
Strategic Community Engagement Step 3:
Get the Community (Resources) into the School
and the School into the Community

- Relationships with the community are paramount! Be creative and think out of the box, especially when soliciting community members for resources.

6

"Doing the Most" to Make Our School a "Normal" School

Transforming Student Culture, Climate and Discipline

As I mentioned before, my first introduction to this beloved community high school when I visited as a guest was not one that left a favorable impression on me. It was like walking onto a movie set! What I saw was so unbelievable that I thought what I was seeing simply couldn't *possibly* be real.

First of all, the facility itself was an old, unkempt, broken-down school building that looked like a war zone. In fact, I called it "Beirut." It was really loud and rowdy. There were at least 75 kids standing around in the hallways, just chilling with their friends. There were kids coming back to the campus from Popeyes, walking back into the school with boxes of chicken like it was normal, acceptable routine. Some of the kids were in the hallway kissing and openly making out. There were kids hanging out and talking about what they had done the weekend before, and the teachers were standing there talking with them. There was a police officer in the hallway talking to a kid while the other officers were just sitting in their office. Mind you, this wasn't between periods during the transition to class; all of this was happening *during* class time! The kids had absolutely no intention of going to class. None whatsoever. Zero. *Nada*. What's worse, teachers and staff saw these things happening. I thought to myself, *This cannot be happening!* At the time that I visited as a guest, no one could have told me that this out-of-control school would later become my school.

Fast forward to three years later, when I was hired to be the new principal of the high school in April 2017. It was officially my school, but by this point, the campus was in jeopardy of being closed for good. Everything was still the same except the facilities. When I'd visited the campus as a guest a few years before, the building was in disrepair. Now, the district was building the school a new campus facility, which was only half finished by the time I began as principal. Knowing that I was going into a newer facility gave me some hope; I thought that with the new building would come new behaviors. However, this was not the case.

While there were some slight changes that accompanied the newer facility, everything else was basically the same as it was when I'd visited as a guest a few years before. The first day that I walked into the school as the new principal, I saw about 35 kids standing around in the hallways during class time, and no one had a pass to be out of class. When I looked into the rooms at the kids that were in class, I saw a lot of them on their phones. Also, as I'd observed years before as a visitor, there were still kids walking out the front door of the school. Nothing had changed.

I remember asking one of the kids who was leaving the building, "Sweetheart... where are you going?"

"Oh, I'm done with school for today."

"Okay. So how would anybody know that you're done with school? Do you have a badge on that says that you leave early?" I would ask.

He said, "No, Miss. We don't wear badges."

There were kids walking into the building at 10:30 a.m. – hours after the first bell – for school, and I had no idea if they were students or not because they weren't wearing badges. Everything seemed to be in complete disarray. There was no order. There appeared to be minimal control on the campus, and the school was failing miserably. Years before, when I visited the campus as a guest, these were things that I witnessed at which I shook my head and thought, *Something needs to be done about this!* Now, as the new principal, these were my problems to solve.

My goal was to turn around the school and make it a success, but the plan had to begin with culture transformation. I knew that unless I changed the culture, I couldn't change the school, so as soon as I took the reins as principal, I began to make immediate changes to the campus culture. As I've explained, I knew I had to act quickly to establish a first impression; I needed to establish up front that there was going to be control and order on the campus under my leadership. You can probably imagine how much of a culture shock occurred once I immediately began making these changes. The new standards and expectations for how to conduct oneself on campus were, in many cases, unwelcomed changes. However, for the success of the kids, the school's culture had to shift!

Culture Transformation Message 1: Dress for Success!

As the principal, I feel it's necessary that I serve as the model for dressing for success on the campus. I feel that my attire and overall self-presentation sends a message to the kids, the teachers, the staff, and everyone who sees me. This is a message that communicates that I am professional, intentional, and a serious leader who means business coupled with a sense of style. I try my best to look professionally daily; I either wear a business suit or a dress. I rarely dress casually, and I never wear jeans to work. I wear heels, usually 4 or 5-inches, daily and before you wonder how, my blessing and curse is that I have my father's feet! In any case, I'm rarely in flats because I'm only 5'4" – and I think heels help me communicate with a little more authority! I would be looking up at the kids' nose hairs in my high school if I wasn't wearing heels, so aside from making me look like a professional, heels help to level the playing field, allowing me to look at my shorter kids eye-to-eye. When I first became their principal, my kids would ask, "Miss, if a fight breaks out, can you catch us in those heels?" I would look them in the eye, smile, and say, "Try me!"

When I arrived at the school, the students had on pants that sagged so low that their behinds were showing. The girls wore satin sleeping bonnets, headscarves, and flip flops. Some of the boys had jackets on with no shirt underneath and had the jacket zipped all the way down with their chest showing. I would say, "You have no shirt on! Where did you think you were coming today? The club?" They would respond, "Miss, we don't have to wear a shirt here," with a completely straight face, totally convinced that what they were saying was the gospel truth. I would just look at them in disbelief. This was truly unbelievable.

If you remember, some of the kids at the school formerly had been my students at the middle school when I was the principal there. I would see these kids, pull them aside and ask, "Hey! What's going on here? Why are you dressed like that? Why aren't you in dress code? You know this wouldn't happen if you were with me!"

They would reply by saying, "Oh, they don't care what we wear here. We can wear whatever we want! They don't say anything."

After that, I would tell them that my expectation was that they start complying with the dress code – a dress code that they knew but that they just chose not to abide by, because before, there were no consequences if they didn't.

One of the first things that I knew I had to address to turn around the campus culture was the dress code. Our kids looked the way they looked because they were not respecting the fact that this was an institution of learning, so a certain decorum was expected. I was intent on providing them with these parameters, always emphasizing the importance of not dressing for where you are, but for where you want to be. Wherever you envision for yourself going in the future, dress the part today!

As soon as I came on board, I made an announcement over the PA system: starting Monday, the school dress code would be enforced, no exceptions. I didn't drastically change the dress code; I knew that going to the standard school uniform of khaki pants and a collared shirt in one of two colors wouldn't work, because most of our students didn't have the resources to go out and buy them. To implement such a drastic change and require full compliance would be to fight an uphill battle. Instead, we made a suitable compromise and set an attainable standard for the dress code. The students were to begin wearing a collared shirt that was either black, green, white or yellow (the school colors are green and yellow, but I added in black and white to increase their options). They were also allowed to wear jeans instead of just khakis; however, the jeans could not be ripped or have any holes above the knee. Additionally, I banned the wearing of flip flops, satin bonnets, headscarves and do-rags. We wanted to increase the level of professionalism and presentation among our kids so they would be clear that they were dressed for school, not the club, not the gym or the grocery store.

Understanding that the kids wouldn't be successful in adapting to the dress code without the support of their parents, I ensured that we made phone calls to the parents. First, we notified them that this was not a new dress code; as the new principal, I was just going to begin enforcing the dress code that was already in place. Then, we shared the details of the dress code, including what was allowed, when reinforcement would begin, and what the consequences would be if their child came to school in violation of the dress code. Of course, we received some pushback from the parents.

"It's the end of the year! Y'all just now starting the dress code? That don't make no sense!"

We would calmly explain, "No, Ma'am. There's been a dress code. Your child just hasn't been following it. Now, they are going to be required to follow it."

I had a lot of these conversations with parents. However, I was okay with it, because I knew that what we were doing was setting the stage for the turnaround. As the new principal, it was important for me to make an immediate impact on the campus by making immediate efforts to put things in order. We had to make it clear that things were already changing at the school, even though it was the end of the year. We continued to enforce the dress code throughout the month of May. Then, over the summer break, we allowed some of the students to come to campus and help us create the dress code for the upcoming school year.

For teachers, I required that they dress like they were coming to work to teach. Far too many of them presented themselves as overly-casual, sloppy, and unprofessional. I explained to them that because we were requiring the kids to comply with a more professional dress code, the teachers would have to pick up their game, too.

> *Dr. Campbell is a servant, graceful and authentic leader. Her energy and presence speak volumes and are contagious. I remember meeting her and thinking how graceful she was. When I started working for her, I witnessed her brilliance and servitude. She leads from the back and creates the foundation for everyone to build themselves to the best versions of themselves. Her agenda has never been herself. She gives an authentic space for her teachers, staff, and students. When I first met her, I was captured by the heels, but when I saw her kick them off to race a student down the hallway, I knew then that she was different. The kids knew she was, too.*
>
> – B. Jackson, Science Teacher

Culture Transformation Message 2: Come to School!

Campuses like ours tend to have a lot of absences – significantly more than schools in more affluent districts tend to have. There are myriad reasons why kids in underserved communities tend to be absent from school. For example, we found the following to be the primary reasons that our kids stayed at home:

- Some kids would allow a minor sickness, like a stomachache, to keep them at home.
- Some kids would be very sick and not have any health insurance, so they couldn't see a doctor.
- Some kids' lives were so complicated that they were mentally exhausted and could not function, so they stayed home.
- Some kids would have to babysit younger siblings.
- Some kids had young kids of their own and had to stay at home with them.

- Some kids didn't want to walk to school or stand at the bus stop when the weather was bad.

- Some kids just skipped school, telling their parents they had gone to school, when they actually had not.

A large part of our campus culture transformation plan was to address these issues so that we could encourage our kids to come to school. Some parents had become so used to allowing their kids to stay home from school for the littlest reasons. Neither the parents nor the kids realized just how much not being at school affected their education. In fact, the number of school days missed is the number one factor in a kid's ability to pass an end-of-course exam like the STAAR test. Thus, we had to do the work of helping both the parents and students understand that if the kids were going to be successful at school, they had to stop allowing any little excuse to keep them at home. In order to succeed in school, they had to *show up* to school. As soon as the school year began, we put different programs in place to combat our kids not being in school.

First, we told the kids that unless they were seriously sick, they needed to come to school. Sometimes, they didn't show up for school, and when we called them, they said it was because they had a stomachache. Where I'm from, the only way to fix a stomachache is to go to the restroom, so I would tell them to go to the restroom and then come to school. Sometimes, they would say that they were nauseated. Where I'm from, when you feel like you're going to throw up, you drink a Sprite. I would tell them, "Drink a Sprite, and let's go!" Of course, if they were *truly* ill, they stayed home.

Then, there were the more pressing issues that we had to deal with that kept students out of school, like being sick and not having health insurance to see a doctor. Well, guess what? We had a clinic on the school campus! We told students who were in this position that instead of staying home, the best thing for them to do was to come to school and go to the clinic. The clinic could diagnose them, treat them, give them an over-the-counter medication to take, or write a prescription for them, if necessary. The clinic also gave vaccinations, and it had specialists that came in, like orthopedic doctors, once every two weeks. We made sure that we educated parents about having a clinic located on campus that was a one-stop shop, which removed excuses for their kid to have to miss school, unless under written doctor's orders to stay at home. We have all played hooky at one time or another, but having 12, 24, or 58 absences was unacceptable.

There were also cases in which we realized that some of our kids, who went through a lot because of the context in which they lived, were not able to express their feelings. They kept everything inside without any outlet. Because of this, they were just mentally and emotionally overwhelmed and exhausted. Some days they just couldn't bring themselves to get out of bed and make it to school. When we learned that kids were dealing with this, we would refer them to the on-campus psychiatrist, which was also present in our on-campus clinic. We would also send them to our Communities in Schools program, because they provided services for kids with mental and emotional issues by connecting them with a counselor or therapist who would treat them, and usually for free.

Another issue that we had to address in helping our kids to be able to come to school was childcare. Sometimes, their parents had to go to work and didn't have anyone to babysit their younger children, so they required their high school kids to stay home and take care of them. Then, there was the issue of our kids having kids of their own at home. They might not have daycare for their smaller children, or if any of their children got sick on a school day, the student wouldn't have anyone to watch them. To remedy this, we connected the students with our Communities in Schools program, or our school nurse who helped our students receive free childcare services for those who had kids.

Then, there was the transportation issue; kids did not want to walk to school or stand at the bus stop when the weather was bad. In these cases, we made sure that they had transportation; we would arrange for transportation. When I first came on as principal of the school in April 2017 (during the last two months of the school year), I borrowed a golf cart from another local high school. The principal of that school, Mr. Fuentes, was nice enough to let me borrow one of his. By the summer, our school had purchased two golf carts of our own. We'd roll around the neighborhood every day in our carts, rounding up students. We just needed them at school.

Finally, there was the biggest issue; the kids just skipped school because they were able to get away with doing so. Their parents left for work early in the morning and came home late in the evening, so they didn't know if their kids were going to school or not. When their kids skipped school, they never found out about it. To address this issue and make sure that parents knew that their children were not at school, we made sure that we had attendance case workers. Any kid who was absent for three days would get a home visit from our attendance case worker, and the case worker would have a face-to-face conversation with the parent.

Having active, involved attendance case workers played a big role in helping us get our students back in school. Mr. Provost, who was a staple in the community, knew everyone's parents and family and knew how to make contact! As soon as I came on board as principal, in addition to having the assistant principals move their desks into the hallway, I also had the attendance clerks move their desks in the hallway. This way, working together, we could monitor which kids were at school and in class vigilantly. Then, we started making phone calls to parents immediately, once we noticed that their kids weren't in school. With their help, we got their kids back into school.

We made every effort to add some type of system or program to combat everything that was keeping students from coming to school. Did it work 100%? No, but it raised our attendance about 8% in the first year, which was huge. Because our funding was connected to our attendance rate, this meant at least an extra $500,000 for the campus budget. This was important because it allowed us to do more for the kids that we served.

Culture Transformation Message 3: Get to Class!

My pet peeve is kids in the hallway. Kids should not be in the hallway, because if they're in the hallway, they're not learning. Period. One of our primary messages, as we attempted to change our campus culture was that it was not okay to be in the hallway. Get to class! To enforce this, at times, all of my staff members' desks were moved to the hallways, including assistant principals and attendance clerks to keep a watchful eye on who's in the hallways and what's happening in the hallways.

It's important for the kids to know that someone is always watching them. For example, sometimes, we would get word that something big was going on at the apartments nearby. We would automatically know that we might have a rough day on campus, because all of the kids involved in whatever was going on went to our high school. On those days, it was all hands on deck! Every five feet, you would see an adult in the hallway, and we would maintain this presence all day long. We were there to make sure that the kids peacefully navigated the hallways and went straight to class instead of starting some drama. There's not much that a kid can get into when there are so many adults watching.

Having my staff constantly monitoring the hallways helped us to nearly eliminate kids being out of class and walking around. It also cut down on a lot of kids disrupting class and then having to go to the principal's office and wait for 30 or 45 minutes to see someone. Instead, the assistant principals were right there in the hallways to handle the kids immediately. All that the teacher had to do was open the door, ask for the assistant principal to come, and the issue would be addressed on the spot. This ensured that the students didn't miss so much class time when they were being dealt with for discipline issues.

On my first visit to the high school in 2015, I remember parking next to a car riddled with bullet holes. I immediately wondered if I'd made the right decision to help in what was called one of the "most dangerous neighborhoods in America." As I stepped inside the school, I wondered how kids could learn in an environment that seemed so depressing and forgotten. We stood in the halls and watched the students nonchalantly come and go as they pleased throughout the day. They often showed up in pajamas and slippers or whatever they slept in overnight. Many students took their time going to class and would linger in the hallways until they were ready to participate. Others didn't even bother to go to class at all. When I asked one of the adults why this wasn't being addressed, the response was, "We pick and choose our battles here." I believe some of the adults were truly afraid of the kids.

A little over a year after we started Lighthouse for Students at the school, we noticed major changes taking place. The district tore down one side of the building and rebuilt it. There was a new administration with a very focused new principal. Dr. Campbell-Rhone came in with a bang! Dress code came into effect and students started wearing appropriate clothing. The halls emptied when the bell rang. Students were in class on time; they would panic if they were running late knowing their classroom door would shut and they would have to go to the office. The halls were quieter, brighter and had sayings on them. Incentives were given and the kids enjoyed the rewards. I can't emphasize enough how significant the impact was, not only on the students, but even the staff was lifted by the respect that was being shown in the school. It was a pleasure to watch the students meet expectations and set goals that will change generations.

- Kelly Martens, Lighthouse for Students

Culture Transformation Message 4:
Mind Your Manners!

Many of our kids, as many kids do, did not display the best manners. We knew that as we prepared our kids to go out into the world after high school, we couldn't just send them out with education; we had to send them out with some social skills. By teaching our kids these skills, we were not only helping them to become more socially acceptable for the future, but we were also helping to develop a present campus climate that was kind, polite, and pleasant.

For example, we established a number of new protocols, like requiring the teachers to greet students at the door with "Good morning," or "Hello," and address the students by name as they entered the classroom. We also expected the kids to reciprocate and corrected them when they didn't do so. This helped the kids to develop the basic social skill of saying "Good morning," when they encountered someone rather than walking into a room without saying a word. We taught our kids the importance of responding with "Yes, ma'am," and "No, ma'am," and "Yes sir," and "No sir." Many of them were not used to having to address adults this way. We emphasized the necessity of saying "Please," "Thank you," "Excuse me," and other niceties, all of which were expected of them daily. Additionally, we taught them basic courtesies like looking people in the eye when talking to them. Over and over again, we had to train our kids by saying, "I'm talking to you. Look at me. I'm over here. Talk to me." Some of the kids weren't accustomed to doing any of this before because they weren't held accountable for doing so. They had no idea that, up until now, they had been missing basic courtesies. However, we loved them enough to teach them to operate as their best selves.

In addition to teaching the kids how to relate to others politely and respectfully, we also taught them how to relate to themselves. We no longer let them walk around the school with their heads down. When we would see them in this posture, we would say, "Pick your head up! There's nobody on the ground talking to you!" We taught our kids to function with a sense of significance and dignity, to believe that they were more and act like they *were* more because they were more. This was a big, difficult pill for many of our kids to swallow because their old way of operating was all they knew. However, as difficult as it was to get the pill down, they swallowed it. They embraced the changes, and in doing so, changed themselves. I couldn't be any prouder of them.

Culture Transformation Message 5:
Let's Do Whatever It Takes to Get You Graduated!

On my very first day as the new principal of the school, a student – a high school senior – came to my office asking to see the new principal. There were fewer than two months left in the school year, and she wanted me to answer one question for her: was she going to graduate? She also had a twin sister who attended school with her. Both girls were beautiful young ladies, who, although similar with their identical faces and short, thin build, were different. They were like yin and yang. The twin who was most concerned about whether she was going to graduate or not wore her hair in a long, beautiful, Farrah Fawcett weave. Her sister wore her hair in a short, natural hair style. When they walked into my office, I remember thinking that they were both so gorgeous!

The fact that these girls looked so well put-together would make anyone think that they had everything else in their lives together. This was on the contrary. One of the first eye-opening lessons that I learned on the job that first day was that these kids spent a lot of time making themselves look good on the outside because they were so broken on the inside. Their external appearance was almost like a cover-up for the turmoil that was going on in and around them. I realized that although they looked like functional young adults, they were just broken kids with no direction. It broke my heart to see these two young beauties break down in tears as they sat in front of my desk the first day on the job. It didn't help that I was five months pregnant at the time and already emotional myself. I thought to myself, *I cannot cry on my first day of work.*

I asked one of my assistant principals for their transcripts and reviewed them. I realized that only one of them stood any chance of graduating in May. The beautiful twin with the natural hair was so far behind that there was no way possible that she was going to graduate. When I explained this, she didn't seem surprised; she was living with her boyfriend and rarely came to school, so she had pretty much accepted that graduation was not going to happen for her this year. Her sister with the flowing hair, however, had a chance. She was very close. She had been working so diligently in class, and she had really been trying hard to make sure she did everything necessary to graduate on time. All she wanted to know was whether it was going to happen for her next month. I thought it a tragedy that she had to come seek this information out from her new principal. Why didn't she already have this answer?

I sat down with the twin sister who was close to graduating and did a "side-by-side" with her. I sat her transcript side-by-side next to the list of courses she needed in order to graduate. We realized that she only needed two more classes to graduate. I said, "Listen, love. All you have to have are this class and this class to graduate." She immediately burst into tears.

She said, "Miss, I'm crying for two reasons. I'm crying because you told me this, finally. No one has ever told me what I needed to graduate. Like, I don't even know you! No one has ever taken the time to do something like this with me. And I'm crying because I'm 18 years old, and I'm ready to graduate, but you're telling me I need two more classes! Miss, are you serious?"

I said, "I know that all of this is hard for you to swallow at one time, but here's what we're going to do. We're going to look online and see if we can find these two classes so you can take them online and complete them in time for graduation."

We looked online, and we found the two classes that she needed. Then, I took her directly to the teacher that was in charge of enrolling kids in the online classes. After we enrolled her in the classes, she literally boo-hooed for the next 15 minutes!

I said, "You've got to stop crying! We're going to work the plan, and you're going to be fine!"

"Thank you, Miss! Thank you for everything!" she said. She was so grateful and filled with hope.

When that girl walked across the graduation stage that year, she held on to me, and I to her. She just couldn't believe that she was graduating.

I asked the staff that I began with in April to give me a list of where each senior was, including who was going to graduate and who wasn't. They had no idea. No one was keeping up with the exact numbers of who was passing and who was failing. I was going to have to start from scratch. From there, I ordered every single senior's transcript to be brought to my office immediately. Then, I gathered all of the counselors into one room and had them go over each one of them one by one. Their assignment was to tell me what every one of our seniors was missing for graduation. We put the transcripts of the kids who were missing one or more classes into one pile, and we put the kids who already had everything they needed to graduate into another pile. To my dismay, the sizes of the two piles were almost equal; literally half of our seniors were not on course to graduate the following month. It could have been that they hadn't made up a class that they had failed previously. It could have been that they had too many absences and they needed to make up for the absences. In our school district, if a student has too many absences, they could receive a passing grade in a class, but if they didn't go to class for enough days, they did not get the credit for the class. Instead, they received an "NG" which means "No grade due to excessive absences." If they didn't make up for the time, even though they might have received an A, they didn't get credit towards graduation for it. We had *a lot* of kids in this situation.

Once we determined where each student was, we called each student in, one by one. I sat them down, and I said, "Listen. This is what you have to do in order to graduate. I don't want to see any tears because we don't have time for them right now. We have to go into action so we can get you graduated. This is what I need you to do."

Then, we laid out a plan for how to get them across the finish line in only one month. Beginning in my second week on the job, I asked some of my teachers and staff to stay late every day after school and come in on the weekends – Friday nights, Saturdays and Sundays. They needed to be at the school during these off hours so the kids could be on the computers completing their classes online in record time, and adults needed to be there with them. Everyone had to put in the extra hours – I mean, the registrar, the attendance clerk, the counselors, and all the staff that had anything to do with records.

I said, "Listen. I'm going to have these kids here Friday, Saturday and Sunday, and every day after school. I need you all to be prepared to take these kids in and sit with them while they do their computer classes online. They're going to need your support. Starting tomorrow, you need to plan for 100 to 125 kids to show up, ready to do the extra work."

The teachers and staff said to me, "We've tried that before. It's not going to work. You think that these kids are going to show up to take those classes? They didn't do it before, and they're not going to do it now, just because you're here. Just because you're the principal now, that's not going to change anything and make them show up!" I wasn't about to let them talk me out of believing I could fix the problems that some of their negligence had caused.

I simply said, "Listen. The kids are going to be here, so I need you to be prepared. Don't worry about what I'm going to do! Make sure you're prepared with 100 to 125 laptops so we can have them ready to go tomorrow."

From there, I handled all of the technical details, like making sure there was a sign-in sheet that the kids used to sign in once they arrived so they could get credit for the attendance. I also ensured that everything else was organized and ready to go. That day, as I was giving instructions, I had to look at eye rolls, listen to grumbles made underneath their breath, and even some staff members continuing to insist aloud, "It's not going to happen! You can prepare all you want, and we can sit here and do whatever you want us to do, but it's not going to happen!"

The next day, 130 kids showed up. The staff and teachers were scrambling, because of course, they didn't think that the kids were going to be there, so they didn't do everything I'd instructed them to do in order to be prepared. Those kids were so excited about coming to fix their grades, to fix their attendance and to graduate! There were even some kids who I had not met with, mostly because they weren't at school, who showed up the next day. They had just heard via word of mouth from the other kids that they might be able to catch up and graduate in a month. The message was, "Hey, come tomorrow! You can fix your credits, you can do your attendance recovery for the days you missed, and you can graduate in May!" This word of mouth encouragement worked. In fact, it got kids back in school who hadn't been in a while, because they now had clear direction on the path towards graduation. They showed up because there was hope.

I think that this big initiative to successfully get our seniors graduated was the most pivotal piece in showing that we were about to make a change at our school. It also made a clear dividing line and made each teacher and staff member pick a side. Either you were going to be a part of the turnaround, or you weren't. Either you were going to put in a whole lot of extra and work hard for these kids, or you weren't. If you weren't, you were going to say goodbye on your own or be asked to do so. You were not going to be allowed to just stay around and get paid.

This initiative and its resultant success also sent some clear messages to the students. The first message: this new principal is somebody who cares about us. The second message: but, she is demanding! They were right on both accounts. At that time, my two new APs and I had called in each and every senior and personally met with them one-on-one. We had personally called their parents and said, "Look. We've got to get this child graduated in a month, and this is what needs to happen." We called, wrote letters to and texted bosses that said, "Listen, this student is scheduled to work tomorrow, but she also has to graduate in a month. I know that you know that graduation is more important than anything in this child's life. I need you to let her off of work so she can do what she needs to do in order to graduate." The bosses let my kids off their jobs so they could work on making up their credits and attendance.

When I began as principal in April, less than 50% of our students were prepared to graduate. After we sprang into action, developed a plan for each senior who needed extra support to graduate, we increased this number to about 90%. This helped to establish, among the students, teachers, staff, school district, and community, that we meant business. We made an immediate impact and got immediate, measurable results!

Culture Transformation Message 6: Work with Us, and We'll Work with You!

I was prepared to do whatever we needed to do to help everyone win – the teachers, the staff, the parents, and the kids. As long as they were willing to work with me and my team, we would work with them to help them succeed. However, it couldn't be a one-sided equation; we couldn't do our part without their cooperation, if they were going to succeed.

We communicated this message to as many people as possible as often as possible. For example, we called the parents to let them know when their child wasn't at school, if their child was having discipline issues, and if their child wasn't doing well in classes. If the parents would work with us by reinforcing our policies, putting consequences in place for poor behavior and supporting the kids with what they needed for school, together, we could help the child achieve success. However, if we were doing our part at the school and we didn't have the parent's cooperation in working with us, they couldn't expect the best outcome.

We also weren't going to allow the teachers and staff on the campus to lose. Not all of our kids were what would be considered "out of control," "excessively disruptive" or "problem kids." There were only a handful of kids who fit this category, disrupting classes, not listening to the staff members, and wreaking havoc in the school. I knew that in order for the teachers and staff to feel supported, I was going to have to deal with these kids. We were not going to allow two or three kids to destroy the culture that we were trying to build on our campus. We would pull them out of class, if necessary. We were on the phone with their parents constantly. We talked on the phone to their probation officers. We had meetings with them and sent them to professional counseling. We did everything we could before we would send them off to an alternative school or suspend them. We tried to make it very clear to our parents that we were working with them and their kids, but at the same time, we were not going to allow their kids to completely change the climate of the campus that we were trying to develop.

Dr. Campbell touched everything at the school. If there was a fight, she was there. Professional learning community? She was there. Cafeteria duty? She was there. Data meetings? She was there. Planning for student outcomes? She was there. Events for the elementary and middle schools that fed into our school? There. Games? There. Walkthroughs? There. Community

> meetings? *There. Attendance meetings? There. Home visits? There. She was there, keeping her finger on the pulse of every-thing at the school.*
>
> – L. Villareal, School Attendance Clerk

Culture Transformation Message 7: There's a Whole *World* to Explore Out There!

Our kids often lacked exposure. For many of them, all they know is their neighborhood. In fact, some will go through life and grad-uate high school and never leave outside of a ten-mile radius of their neighborhood. They may never leave their zip code. However, I understand the value of exposure for young people. It broadens their worldview and helps them aspire to experience more in life. It increases their perception of their own potential by showing them what they can become. Most of all, each exposure experience shows them a new and different aspect of the world and helps them understand that there's so much more to see and do outside of their neighborhood. Exposure births aspirations in them to ex-plore all that the world has to offer, because there's a whole world to explore out there. The more they experience, the more they real-ize how big the world really is and how many great opportunities it holds for them. Academics alone won't bring them success; they must have exposure. Exposure matters.

Knowing that our school budget was nothing like that of schools in more well-off neighborhoods, we have really been blessed with people who donated funding for our kids to have experiences that they might not otherwise have had. For example, they paid for our kids to go on college tours, and even to go to plays and to nice restaurants after school as rewards for work well done. One of our biggest exposure opportunities was when Mrs. Jolivet-Gronski took the kids in our robotics class to an event at a Fortune 500 robotics company in San Francisco. The kids literally cried on the airplane because they were so emotional about leaving Houston, being on a plane, and traveling to another state. They had never been out of their neighborhood before, let alone to an entirely different state! We were fortunate enough to capture priceless video footage of our kids crying, simply because they were overwhelmed with the idea that they finally got to go somewhere. They finally got to leave their neighborhood. Nowadays, they make me laugh with how they very casually and nonchalantly go back and talk about traveling to San Francisco like it's something that they do frequently. I count it all as blessings that we were able to facilitate our kids having such experiences. They might not be able to say that they went to Dubai or Paris for their birthday (like the kids used to tell me when I was teaching at my first middle school), but they can surely say that they've been out of state.

Culture Transformation Message 8:
Hard Work Has Its Rewards!

One of the things that we wanted to do in order to change the culture on the campus was to emphasize to our kids that when they worked hard, their hard work and effort would not only be seen and recognized, but it would be rewarded. As I explained before, the community stepped up to provide our school with donations that we would use to incentivize and reward desired student behaviors. We would attach rewards to improved standardized test scores, high classroom achievement, and other desired behaviors that we wanted to encourage and incentivize. Additionally, we would do drawings with the kids and offer all kinds of little things as prizes and rewards throughout the school year. This on-going reward system kept them engaged and looking for opportunities to earn more and more of these perks, and this resulted in them striving to do more and do better.

The reward system that I put into place had a really big impact on how willing our kids were to give all they had. By the time I came on board as principal, the kids had gone so long without recognition of the work that they were doing that they were desperate for someone to come in and simply say, "Job well done!" or "I see your hard work, and I appreciate your effort!" Instead of such affirmation, they had become accustomed to hearing, "Y'all are just dumb kids," or "Y'all haven't been successful in forever, so I don't know if you can do it." Therefore, for us to come in and say, "Hey, y'all are really smart kids! I know you can do it, and this is what I'm going to give you if you do," was groundbreaking! I think that the system of recognition and rewards that I established in the school became both the extrinsic and intrinsic motivator for our kids to strive to do better. It led to a student culture that said, "Finally, somebody's recognizing that I'm doing something really good, and on top of that, I get rewarded for it!"

Our rewards system was primarily based upon "Campbell's Cash," a dollar-style piece of paper that students could earn for a job well done. For each "Campbell's Cash" bill they received, students could purchase snacks from the school snack store (which I kept stocked with cases and cases of chips, drinks and other snacks donated by my contacts in the community) when it opened after school. They could also use Campbell's Cash to purchase necessities like school supplies. Some students opted to save up their Campbell's Cash for a bigger prize rather than spending their bucks immediately. For example, they could use $5 of Campbell's Cash to purchase a pair of socks or a make-up bag, or they could save up their hard-earned school cash to enter a drawing for various electronics.

Our kids absolutely loved the opportunity to earn these bucks and exchange them for the things they wanted. We loved the Campbell's Cash because it offered great motivation to the students to do their best. For example, our kids were supposed to have their school-assigned laptops every day. Sometimes, my assistant principals and I would just walk through the cafeteria and give everybody who had a laptop a school dollar.

We rewarded our kids for everything. We rewarded them for good SAT scores, for good report card grades, for being inducted into the National Honor Society, and so much more. We strived to provide whatever motivated them and made them want to work harder. We rewarded them with all kinds of stuff. We wanted to let the kids know that if they did well, as leaders, we were going to go out of our way to make sure they were rewarded for a job well done.

One of the most important aspects of our system of rewards was that we did not only reward the big accomplishments; we also rewarded those things that many would consider to be small. For example, during standardized testing time, we made it clear to our kids that we were competing against all of the other schools. After the tests were finished and the district released the scores, if we beat the other schools' scores, our entire school would get really excited about it. I would get on the PA system in the morning and make an announcement, telling them all of the other schools that we beat.

Rather than coming up with my own ideas of what would be good rewards for our kids, I was always sure to ask them "What is it that you want as a reward?" This helped to ensure that they were getting exactly what they wanted instead of what I wanted for them. Knowing that they would receive a specific reward that they'd asked for gave them further incentive to get the job done and achieve their goals. Sometimes, the students would ask me for what I considered major rewards – big things, like trips to an amusement park. When they asked for things like this, however, I didn't say "No." Instead, I would say, "Look, if you want something that big, you're going to have to give me 80 percent!" Then, because they really wanted this reward, they would really strive for 80 percent. Sometimes they achieved their goal, and sometimes they didn't. Either way, I didn't make the reward system all or nothing. I didn't set up a system where if they met the specific goal, they got the reward and if they didn't meet the specific goal, they didn't get the reward. We never made it to Disneyland, but I always evaluated their effort and rewarded hard work.

> For [the school's] students to raise their academic performance in the face of those struggles is remarkable. They had a lot of help from a dedicated staff led by Principal Khalilah Campbell-Rhone. [Their] educators understand that improving inner-city schools means more than teaching and testing. It means addressing the needs of the whole child and creating an environment where learning is possible.
>
> As a city, we need to understand that society's problems don't stop at the schoolhouse doors. Academic progress only comes if we confront all of the issues that make it difficult for children to learn, just as they have done at [this school].
>
> – Ken Wells, President and CEO, Cherish Our
>   Children International/No More Victims, Houston

If we set a goal and the kids were really working hard towards it but didn't reach it, they received a scaled-down version of the reward they wanted. They would say, "Okay, okay. We know we didn't do what we were supposed to, but thank you for what you did!" This appreciation for someone meeting their basic needs of recognition and rewards fostered levels of effort and determination in our kids that they had never demonstrated before, ultimately resulting in their unprecedented success.

Culture Transformation Message 9: Someone Is *Always* Here for You!

When working with kids who come from our community, mentorship is important. Many of our kids find it difficult to find positive role models who they can look at and aspire to become like, and even fewer people who can point them in the direction of a successful future. I have had some of my kids come to me and actually say, "I don't have a mentor or anyone to look out for me, so I know that I'm only going to be able to do this or that in life." For every one of my kids that admits something like this to me, I know that there are dozens of others who feel the same way. The sad reality is that the vast majority of my kids didn't have someone to reach out to for help. I also know that without mentors exposing them to greater potentials of what they could do and become, the kids' notions of what they could do and become in life would be extremely limited. Recognizing this, one of the most effective programs that I knew I had to put in place at the school was a mentoring program.

I knew that I didn't have enough people on my staff to serve as mentors for all of the kids who needed that special someone that was there just for them – that someone to talk to, to ask a question to or to get advice from when it was needed. Really being there for kids to give them the attention and focus that they needed would take time and focus that my hard-working staff simply did not have. Thus, we began working really hard on getting each and every kid in the school a mentor.

Another one of the biggest efforts that was made in this direction was honing on a new position in the district called "Wraparound Specialist." Tondelyn made sure that students had clothes, food, and metro bus tickets. She also supported our mentorship program, provided outside resources for the students, and supported the majority of campus events.

Another group that we wanted to ensure that our kids knew was there for them, as friends and not foes, was the local law enforcement. Because of all of the news stories permeating the media about the disproportionate numbers of arrests and killings of young Black and Hispanic males, it was no secret that there were major issues between them and law enforcement officers. Having two Black sons made me hyper-sensitive to this issue! One of the things that I wanted to do was build a bridge between our kids and the Houston Police Department (HPD) in order to create a greater sense of trust between them. I wanted the kids to understand that the officers were not always the enemy – and if relationships were formed, they could be their ally.

As a part of this effort, beginning with my first year as principal and continuing, I began bringing HPD officers to the school campus. These police officers were different from the on-site police officers assigned by the school district to patrol and secure the school's campus throughout the day. Our kids viewed the on-campus officers as "school police," even though they were actual licensed police officers. However, the kids viewed HPD officers, the city police, as the enemy. They knew that they would see them at the corner store or the local parks when trouble arose or where danger occurred. My concern was that we could not protect them from troubles when they were away from us, so we had to give them tools to protect themselves.

A funny thing happened the very first year that we brought the HPD officers to campus. I made a scheduling error that led to me anticipating their arrival one week, when in fact I had scheduled them to come the week before. Without realizing this, I was just walking the hallways of the school, and seemingly out of nowhere, our office began being flooded with calls from people in the community asking, "What happened? What's going on at the school?" The office was sending out radio calls to school staff about all of the phone calls that were coming into the school office from parents. I told them nothing was going on at the school and wondered why they were asking. Then, I went to the front of the school and looked outside. To my surprise, our campus was flooded with HPD officers. Car after car was pulling up, and their cars lined our school building. It was no wonder that everyone was concerned! I apologized profusely to the officers for my scheduling error, and they were good sports about it. Since they were already there, they decided to walk around the school with me that day anyway and agreed to come back the following week.

As we all walked through the school building together, headed to the cafeteria, I kid you not: I had kids running out of the school and away from the building, scaling the fence and running for their lives! They thought that the big team of police officers had come to the school to round up all of the kids who had warrants or who had not been wearing their ankle monitors. I mean, these kids were *flying* out of there! The rest of the kids that remained on campus were no better, ducking off and hiding out from the police officers. I was also saying to myself, "Oh my goodness! I'm going to have 12% attendance with all these kids running away and ducking out today!" After enjoying a good deal of laughter, pulling some kids aside and asking them how they were doing, and having some casual exchanges with the kids who were bold enough to re-main on campus – and visible to our guests – the officers departed. And the students returned.

When the officers returned a week later, you can probably guess that the kids were *not* amused! The kids stopped me in the hallway asking, "Miss... what are you *doing*? Why do you keep bringing the police over here? What are you *doing*?" I told them that the police weren't there to do anything; they just came to visit the students. Despite my assurances that the police were only there for a friendly visit, they said, "Nooo, Miss!" They really thought that we were up to something. This response to any presence of the police was a large part of why we needed to bridge the gap between the students and law enforcement; our kids would never trust the police or understand that the officers were there for them if, at some point, they did not have peaceful, social exchanges with them. Thus, I asked the officers to go into the hallways, and when the bell rang for lunch, just naturally pass by and engage the kids. Just speak to them. I encouraged them to help the kids understand that they were on the kids' side and that they weren't always there to throw them on the hood of a car and arrest them. The purpose was to convince the kids that these officers were there to help them as well. Still, a lot of the kids weren't buying it. As they headed to the cafeteria for lunch, you could hear them whispering, "Who are they looking for?"

In an effort to create an atmosphere that was as non-intimidat-ing as possible, we tried to create more of a party atmosphere in the cafeteria, believing that this would help everyone to let their guards down and facilitate more casual interaction between the kids and police officers. For example, the officers were sitting down and eating with the kids, there were lots of high fives, we had a DJ who had music going in the cafeteria, there was dancing, and there was even an amazing dance off between the officers and the kids! It was a wonderful time. One of the local television news stations heard there were excessive officers on campus and sent a crew. Shocked by what they saw, they filmed the event and ran it later that day on the evening news and on Facebook.

By the end of things, these kids, who hated the police and called them "pigs," felt a greater sense of connection to and a different type of relationship with them. They would come to me and say things like, "Oh, I saw Officer Johnson on the street the other day!" The beauty was that when they saw the officers in the streets now, rather than fear and run from them, they gravitated to them, feeling like they had an ally rather than an enemy. In light of the success of this program, we continued to bring it to our campus each year.

The following year, we offered a modified version of the program by selecting about 40 boys to sit in the library to talk to a panel of police officers, because these boys were the types of kids who needed to develop a deeper understanding of law enforcement officers the most. As members of my staff and I sat in the room and supervised, the officers on the panel asked the students questions like, "What are you afraid of?" "What is it that keeps you up at night?" "What would you want if you could fix your neighborhood?" As they asked these questions, the kids were completely quiet; they barely spoke a word in response. The officers looked up at me and my staff and said, "All you ladies, get out. We've got this!" At first, I was reluctant, but then I remembered what it was we were trying to do in bringing the officers to the school: build bridges and help the students establish a relationship with them that could, potentially, one day save their lives. My female staff and I left the room and stood outside. We were looking into the glass windows like a parent who had dropped their baby off at daycare for the first time as we tried to figure out what they were saying. Turns out, the officers had some good, dynamic and real conversations with the kids, and once again, it was a really awesome event. By the end of it, our boys felt that they had another level of support in the community and that they weren't all alone out there.

In November 2018, 19 African American women ran for judge in Harris County [in Houston], and all 19 of them won. It made national news. Dr. Campbell thought it would be great to bring them in to talk to the girls, so in December, we had 12 of the 19 judges speak to 55 of our young ladies. These young ladies were hand-picked by administrators and teachers. They weren't necessarily the best behaving female students; some were, but others were those that were like... they definitely needed a mentor, someone who could see something more in them than they saw in themselves. We had the young ladies dress up, and if they didn't have nice clothes, Dr. Campbell and Ms. Judge went out and purchased clothes for them so they could participate. They spent time with the judges and had a very nice lunch sponsored by a local business. The young ladies were able to have one-on-one conversations with these judges, the majority of which attended historically-black colleges and universities. They came from neighborhoods not unlike Sunnyside. Some were from single-parent families who never knew their mother, father or either parent, and others had parents who were in prison. Their willingness to share their stories of how they overcame the odds to be successful made a big impact on our young ladies. That is one of many activities we implemented for our girls. Dr. Campbell is not just about discipline and consequences; she's also about helping the students change and transform into better versions of themselves.

– T. Hampton, Assistant Principal

Culture Transformation Message 10: Leave the Drama at the Door!

Working with students like ours over the years has taught me some important lessons, one of which was that nothing distracts from a student's ability to focus on learning like drama. It was no surprise to me that our campus was *full* of daily drama. I knew that I would have to turn this aspect of the campus culture around, because if I didn't, all of the initiatives I was putting into place to help them achieve academically would be futile. How can a kid focus on learning when a fight is breaking out in the hallway or the cafeteria with every other class period change? Even worse, how can students focus on the teacher in front of them when they know that there is a possibility that students near them may 'blow' if they become too agitated?

I had to be the first to establish that such behavior was no longer acceptable. It was time to leave the drama at the door and focus on what they were there for: an education. Drama seemed to thrive on a campus like ours; the different sociological factors present among the student body on our campus could combine to create a recipe for a perfect dramatic storm at any given moment. I could tell story after story about the various types of dramatic situations that have occurred among the students on our campus. We've had students that were questioned for murder, former students that were killed in police gun battles, students shot at parties over the weekend, aggravated assaults, you name it, it has affected us.

We did all we could at school to help our kids navigate the drama they experienced outside of school, but it was difficult. I mean, think about it. We told kids every day to focus, pass the end-of-course exam, succeed in school and graduate. However, how effective could this message really be when there's so much unbelievable drama going on in the child's life? The dichotomy was glaring:

at home, things were crazy and filled with all kinds of unthinkable goings on, but at school, we expected the student to be normal and focus on preparing for a test! There were so many different pieces to the puzzle when trying to effectively educate our kids, so many that they alarmed me every day. I don't know how some of them could wear the masks they do. However, all my staff and I could do at the school was try to eliminate as much of the drama as we could from the school culture so that when our students did come to campus, it was as "normal" of an environment as possible. They needed at least one place in their lives to escape to that was drama free.

Eliminating the drama that was so common in our campus culture meant showing the kids, from the very beginning, that I wasn't going to just be an invisible figurehead sitting in an office and calling the shots from behind closed doors. Instead, I wanted them to see that I was an involved, invested, accessible and visible leader who was there to lead the school in a completely different direction than it had been going before. I made sure that I walked around the school constantly and that I was always visible in the hallways. I was everywhere and I saw everything, so they knew not to try anything shady in my presence. I wasn't a silent observer; I would either greet them by name, or if I couldn't remember their names, I would call them, "Love" or "Sweetheart." I would also ask them about something they had done the previous day, like taking a test or preparing to do something for a class. I was building a relationship with them. However, in the beginning stages, this relationship was not as a friend; it was as a rule-giver and change agent.

Although I was intentional about interacting with the kids, I didn't do a lot of cheeky "ha-ha" chatter with them when I first arrived. First, it was necessary for them to see me as someone who was coming to bring structure, order, and safety to the campus. They needed to see me as someone who was not going to tolerate the drama anymore, and they would not view me in this way if I came in as the smiling, bubbly principal who was all excited about the kids. Thus, in the initial stages of leading the organization, I wore my "serious hat" every day and kept a straight, but approachable, face that conveyed a clear message: "Don't try it with me!"

I was not the only one responsible for doing away with the drama. My assistant principals were also responsible for coming out from behind their desks and being visible to the students at all times as a deterrent from fighting, arguing, yelling, and other undesired behavior. Also, as I explained before, I hired someone specifically to deal with the culture, climate, and discipline of the students: Assistant Principal Dotson. He did a phenomenal job with helping us remain fair and consistent in discipline and keeping all of the children on their p's and q's as it pertained to discipline.

As an administrative team, we banded together to set the rules and repeatedly reinforced them. It had quickly become clear to the kids that there were new rules in place that were meant to do away with the drama, but this doesn't mean that they began following them immediately. We had to constantly remind them, "This is what we do here. This is what we don't do. This is what we do here. This is what we don't do. No, you're not going to put your hands on someone else; we talk to each other when things don't go our way." Over and over again, they had to be reminded. Yes, it was really exasperating to have to remind someone every five seconds about the new rules of what was acceptable and unacceptable behavior. However, once things caught on, the reinforcement of the "leave the drama at the door" rules took on a life of its own. The kids actually helped to police their peers. They would come to let me, or the APs or the officers know what another kid had done, and we would follow up by investigating the matter and administering discipline, if necessary.

Dr. Campbell wanted to have a Winter Wonderland to give students that fed into our campus holiday gifts. All I could think to myself was, With all that we have to do, why would she add something else to our to-do's? She went on and on about how she wanted our kids to understand how important it was to be a part of giving and not only receiving. She said she wanted to give the younger kids a reason to smile and a reason to be proud of their neighborhood school. So, we went to work... and it turned out amazing. But we knew it would from the time she mentioned it. The crazy thing is, she had us all feeling like it was our idea! We were all involved, staying late and coming early to see kids smile. We enjoyed every moment. And at the same time, she held us responsible for our daily duties.

– P. Barrera, School Secretary

As we did our best to keep our campus a drama-free zone, sometimes, it wasn't the kids that we had to worry about; it was the adults. For example, one day, two ladies were in the main office of the school, yelling at one another at the top of their lungs and looking like they were ready to fight. One of my assistant principals and I had to physically separate them and find out what was going on. After we managed to separate the ladies by taking one outside and leaving the other inside, they were able to calm down, and we got the full story. One of our students, a young girl, had been living with her dad and stepmom for the past year. Apparently, the girl's biological mother, who had been absent from her life for the past two years, had shown up the day before at the dad and stepmom's house saying she was there to take the girl to a dentist appointment – out of the blue! The altercation that occurred between the mom and stepmom in the school office happened the next day. Stepmom and step-grandma had shown up to the school to take the girl home, because they feared that the mom would show up to school and try to take the girl away. The problem was, even though the mom had been out of the picture for years, she still had as much right to pick up the girl as anyone else, because no paperwork had been filed terminating her custodial rights. As a campus, this put us in a touchy situation. We couldn't legally prevent the mom from picking up her daughter, but we also understood that it was the stepmom who had been functioning as the girl's mother for years. As we contacted our legal department, the fight began.

We talked to the girl, and of course, she said she wanted to go home with her stepmom, because that was where her dad lived – where home was – even though she had reluctantly agreed to go to her mom's house the night before since she'd made such a big fuss and put up such a big fight. Now, today, the mom was back to take her home with her again, and she didn't want to go. The girl also disclosed that her mother had someone, who pretended to be an investigator, call her stepmom and tell her that they were coming to pick up the girl and that the girl could not bring her phone with her when her mom picked her up, so there were concerns that the mom might try to disappear with the girl. There were so many other twists and turns to the story that it became one big, drama-filled mess.

It's stuff like this that breaks your heart as a leader. It has nothing to do with school, but it pours over into the school environment and affects the child at school. I say all the time that if adults would get it together, kids would perform! It has everything to do with the adults that are supervising the kids. Unfortunately, we can't change the world. All we can do is focus on what we can influence, and that is our student body. We strive to constantly encourage our kids to do their part to keep our school environment a drama-free zone.

The Result of "Doing the Most": A Changed Culture & Campus Climate

As soon as I came onto the scene as principal at the high school and began making changes to a school culture that had been fixed for years, the word was out, and the buzz began. There was a moment of realization when the students began to say to themselves, "Wait a minute... Now we have rules we have to follow, and we're going to be held accountable for following them?" Before long, the word circulating through the school hallways was that this new principal, Miss Campbell, was "Doing the most!" I was no stranger to this lingo, so I knew exactly what they meant; this is an urban colloquialism used to suggest that a person is doing a lot more than what is standard, or required, for a particular situation. They were right: I *was* doing the most. Why? Because standard approaches wouldn't do in a context like ours, a school that had been failing for nearly a decade and was on the verge of being shut down by the district. I would have to "do the most" in order to get it to where it needed to be in record time... and I did.

Don't get me wrong; it wasn't like they embraced all of the new standards I was putting in place to change the culture with open arms. Everything wasn't always smooth sailing as we sought to establish a new campus climate. This was high school, so of course, there were many bumps in the road and many challenges to overcome. However, my staff and I persisted. I would simply respond by saying, "Yeah, yeah... we are doing the most!" Laugh and keep moving.

My message was unyielding. I would explain, "Yes. This is what we're doing now. We're not going to yell when we walk in the hallway, we're going to pull our pants up, we're not going to wear headscarves and do-rags on our head at school, we're going to wear closed-toe shoes instead of flip flops. Yes, we are going to do *all* of this! You can either enjoy it or not, but you're going to do it." Our message was the same across the board. We'd say it, smile and walk away!

The most difficult part was getting the kids to believe that there was something different than what they knew, and that these new and different ways would work really well for them, if they let them. It was getting them to actually believe us when we said, "No, you're not going to be a dropout. No, you are not going to fail to complete your credits and have to come back next year. No, you're not going to fall into the same cycle of being a dropout and working dead-end jobs, because you are capable of more." However, we encouraged them, they had to join the team and embrace the changes that we were introducing. They had to play their part. In order to get better, we couldn't do better for them; they had to do better for themselves.

As a result of unapologetically "doing the most" from day one it didn't take long to get things under control and begin seeing some changes. In fact, within two weeks of beginning to implement the new culture changes in the school, the students could already feel the culture changing. This spoke volumes. It primarily communicated to me that the students had not only desperately needed structure – they very much wanted it.

In the beginning, the kids called me "Miss" or "Dr. Campbell" or "Principal." However, after the culture changes began to take root, they began calling me "Mama." This switch from being called "Dr. C or Principal" to being called "Mama" was a clear indication that the change that we wanted to happen was occurring. We cared and we showed care by providing structure, discipline, and expectations of them that they had been unaccustomed to having placed on them at school. These same kids, who were accustomed to cursing out their teachers and administrators without a second thought, now respected us at such a high level that they thought of us like kin.

They got to focus on their education, have fun, and live their own lives without having to share in the responsibility of looking after anyone other than themselves. I've always said to the kids, "You get to be a kid here, because every staff member and teacher here is a highly-functioning adult. They can take care of themselves and any adult need on this campus, they don't need your help. You just focus on being a child and leave everything else to us adults." That was hard for them to understand. They were like, *Do what children do? I've always had to be like an adult. I've always had to act grown and help raise my younger siblings. I've always had to work. What do children do?*

Being given the permission to just be a kid and do what kids do was huge. It was a complete reorientation in thinking and in behavior for them. You could almost see the burden lifting off of them as they walked around the campus with dispositions that seemed so much lighter and more carefree. Thus, not only was the campus culture changing as a result of the new rules, structure, order, and expectations, but these changes were also resulting in noticeable changes in our kids' lives.

I'll never forget it. On the first day of school, the fall semester after I became principal, I heard our kids say for the very first time, "Man! We have real rules that we have to follow and *everything*. We go to a *real school* now!" This filled my heart more than words could explain. These kids had equated their previous experience at the school to being something other than a "real school" experience. What they had considered it to be before that time – a fake school, a farce of a school, a substandard organization that didn't measure up as a school – I did not know. What I did know was that it had taken an entire summer of planning how we were going to roll things out, change the culture, prepare for testing, and turn everything about the school around from top to bottom. The changes were drastic, and the kids' perception that we were "doing the most" was accurate. However, our "doing the most" resulted in them getting a "real school." I could not be any prouder of this because these kids deserved a "real school." The fact that they lived in one of the most dangerous zip codes in the nation riddled by poverty and hardship did not make them any less deserving of one.

When Dr. Campbell first got to the school, she asked me to attend an alumni meeting where the Deputy Commissioner was asked to speak. We met in what was called the lecture hall. He sat the community down and explained what would happen when we didn't make it. Dr. Campbell looked him in his eyes and told him that she respectfully disagreed and that she would welcome him back when we were successful. He smirked and told her that that was not likely, but that he'd surely return upon our success. She smirked in return as they shook hands and parted ways. I've worked with her for many years at several different campuses. I knew that we were going to rise to the challenge – period. We planned on the weekends at restaurants, in the evening on campus, we created Campus Bibles, we included alumni and various organizations from No More Victims, the Houston Area Urban League, the Lighthouse, and others who were integral parts of our success in the plan. When we deviated from the plan, she gently (or not so gently) redirected our thinking. The two things she always did – gave credit where it was due and provided what we needed to make the process easier. Everything we did was a joint effort, she just led the way.

– R. Dotson, Assistant Principal

Chapter 6
Transformational Leadership Tips

TLT 6.1
Campus Transformation is the Most Important Thing You Will Do

- When you believe in kids, kids begin believing in themselves.

- Students will rise to the expectations you set.

- What you make important will change.

- Mindset shifts take time and purposeful energy, but it's the most important work you'll do in turnaround.

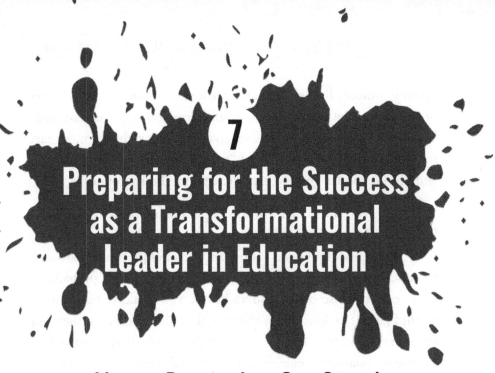

7
Preparing for the Success as a Transformational Leader in Education

Always Remember Our Story!

Up to this point, I've shared all of the gritty details in answer to the question that people have wondered for so long: how did this team come into a school that had been failing for more than a decade, on the verge of being shut down, and turn it completely around in just one year? Hopefully, by reading this story, you have a clear picture of all of the planning, time, commitment, and sacrifices that were required, and how, as a team, we laid it all on the line, stepping up to meet every one of the school's needs in order to give it and the surrounding Sunnyside community what they deserved for years.

Now, before I end, I'd like to address educators directly, particularly those who have embraced the transformational style of leadership, with a proficiency to transform organizations by turning them around. If you are a leader in education seeking to be effective at turning around districts, departments, schools, or any other level of the system, let me warn you: transformation is *not* an easy task. Yet, it can be done. I'm a believer that with the right team, a heart for the people you serve, and a "whatever it takes" mentality, no situation is too far gone to experience a total turnaround.

Whenever you think that a group of people has been losing for so long that there's absolutely no way they can win, remember our story; the school had been losing for years before the turnaround. Whenever you begin to think that you have a low probability of success because other leaders before you couldn't turn things around (and it looks unlikely that you'll be able to do it), remember our story; the school had six different principals in 10 years before I came on board. Whenever you begin to discount the magnitude of what a solid team can do – one that prioritizes the mission over their personal comfort and the size of their paycheck – remember my close-knit, small-but-mighty team of leaders who turned the school around in record time. There were *only six* of us! Whenever you think about walking away and throwing in the towel because change seems impossible for a school or department, remember our story. *Always* remember our story and be encouraged that, despite the odds, transformation is possible.

Whether you are already a principal, or you are an educator who aspires to become a principal who functions according to a transformational style of leadership, I'd like to offer some advice on how to succeed in the role. There are definitely some things that you'll learn only by being on the job each day, but there are other lessons that you can learn from me, saving yourself a lot of time, resources, failure, and disappointment. I encourage you to embrace the lessons and advice that I have to share because I paid a lot for them through my experiences as a transformational leader. After all, why pay the costly price for these lessons yourself when you can get them from me for free?

Before You Enter the Building: 4 Keys to Prepare Principals for Effectiveness as a Transformational Leader in Education

When you become a principal, the assumption is that you're prepared for the job as soon as you go into it. However, I've been in education for 24 years, and I know the truth: most principals who go into the job *are not* prepared for it the first day that they step onto the campus. For the sake of their students and staff, they put on a brave face; they try to look like they know exactly what they're doing, but often, they don't. They're like me. On my first day, I stepped onto the campus with grit, determination and a will to win, but I had to learn all the rest as I went along. I wish I would have had someone come alongside me and share the things with me that I'm sharing with you! It would have made a rocky path a little smoother.

The following represent 4 keys that will help prepare you to be effective as a principal who operates as a transformational leader before you ever enter the building.

Key 1: Toss the Traditional Job Description

If you're a principal going into a school that needs to experience a drastic turnaround, just know that from the very beginning, you're not going to be operating in the traditional role of a principal. Toss that "traditional" job description out of the window because you're going to be doing so much more! Traditional principal job descriptions are what are required of leaders at traditional schools. You are entering into a turnaround school, so what is required of you on the district's formal job description is going to only be a fraction of what you will need to do in order to turn around a school. You'll not only wear the hat of top school leader, but on top of that hat, you'll need to stack on other hats, like coach, referee, analyst, accountant, counselor, motivational speaker, donation seeker, hand shaker, politician, custodian, cheerleader, and the list goes on and on. As you strive to fulfill each of these roles, you'll work longer, you'll work harder, you'll give more, you'll receive less, and if your heart is really in it, you'll love every bit of it.

Key 2: Understand the Operational Context of What You Are Leading

When you're in education, it's easy to assume that students are students and that they are the same from level to level. That is, elementary school is like middle school but with younger kids, and high school is like middle school but with older kids. A lot of leaders go into schools believing that a level is a level, and this is just not true. I can tell you this from experience, as someone who has worked in each of these contexts. They are all quite different, and if you are going to be effective in leading them, particularly if you are tasked with transforming them, you need to know what these differences are. Study and learn about whatever grade you're going into. This is particularly necessary if you have never worked in a high school, and you are dispatched to lead one, because this level of education comes with a lot of details.

There are so many pieces to high school – more than I ever imagined. Principals of high schools need to know about transcripts, guidelines about how long kids need to be in class to receive credit, how many days they have to be present in order to get credit toward graduation, what classes they need in order to graduate, what tests they have to take before they graduate, and if it's possible to graduate if they fail the tests. You need to know things like kids can't be allowed to pick up trash as a form of punishment, can they leave school early if they are sick and need to walk home, kids can only be suspended for a certain amount of days, evaluations have to be done for every kid entering into the special education program, you can't change their placement until there is an ARD, how much time you must be at school during the day to be considered a full-time student and don't you dare begin football practice until UIL says you can, and countless other detailed rules and regulations. You need to know whom you're supposed to call if you have anything from a rodent problem to a leaky roof and keep in mind that there are extracurricular activities – Every. Single. Day. You especially need to know how payroll works, because if any teacher or staff member's money starts running funny, the first person they're going to come to is the principal, and you've got to have a good explanation for them. If your building has renovations anywhere in the school's future, you'll need to lean into the construction learning curve so you can step in as a construction co-manager. When this happened at our school, we held a construction meeting once a week and made decisions about materials, windows, and so many other things about which I'd had no previous knowledge. I found myself Googling things on a daily basis and running to other schools to see what their finishes looked like in order to make sure we had the best of the best at our school. Be sure to add "pseudo architect" to your list of job responsibilities.

You essentially need to know everything that everyone else in the school — counselors, assistant principals, teachers, resource officers, and custodians — knows, but as the principal, you need to know them like the back of your hand. Why? Because when it's all said and done, you're responsible for it all. At the end of the day, you're the leader of the school, and the buck stops with you, so you can't rely on others to know these things for you; you must possess the knowledge yourself. However, don't wait until you're already on the job to learn this knowledge. Once your feet hit the grounds of the campus you've been hired to turn around, you're not going to have time to go back and consult all of the detailed code handbooks because doing so will only slow you down. You also don't want to make uninformed guesses or decisions that violate the codes either. Thus, do yourself a favor and prepare yourself ahead of time. DO NOT RUSH THE POSITION! Before you enter the position, educate yourself on the policies, rules, and regulations.

Key 3: Know the System and Learn How to Work It

Every school system has its own culture, politics, and way of doing things. It could very well be that when you become a leader of a school and see the way the system operates, you might not like it – at all. However, what are you going to do? You're there to turn around a school, not revolutionize an entire school system – that will come later. Whether you like the system and the way it operates or not, you've got to learn how to work it. When I say, "work it," I mean, you have to learn whom you can go to in order to get things you need pushed through, how to approach key individuals in the system (especially the decision makers and resource controllers), what individuals will shoot straight from the hip and tell you the transparent truth about what's happening behind the scenes, what types of events and activities the system smiles upon versus frowns upon, and more. Once you gather this intelligence, learn to work with it. Again, even if you don't like it, don't fight the system; you need to ration your energy, saving the vast majority of it for your students. Do whatever it takes in order to get things done in the system, and then celebrate your wins. If you learn to work the system well enough, those in the system will be celebrating your wins right along with you, highlighting the role that they played in your success!

Key 4: Take the Time to Build Your Career and Learn as You Go

I truly believe that one of the biggest keys to my success as the turnaround principal is that I never really rushed trying to become a principal. I was a school improvement facilitator and an assistant principal before becoming the principal of this beloved community school. A lot of times, people get into the position of assistant principal, but in their hearts, all they really want is to become the principal. They don't take advantage of all that they can learn as assistant principal, and instead, spend a lot of their time gunning for the principal position in their school or another one. While I was assistant principal, I used every minute of it to learn every single thing I could. I stayed focused on my current job of assistant principal, and in doing so, I picked up a wealth of information that would later help me when I accepted a principal position. I was so focused on my current job of assistant principal, in fact, that by the end of my tenure in that role, I felt 'expertish!'

I took the same approach when I was a dean; instead of gunning for the next upward position, I focused my time on learning everything I possibly could as a dean. One of the things that most of my previous supervisors would always say to me was, "You don't need a lot of coaching!" It's because I allowed myself to be coached in all of my prior positions. I brought the wealth of knowledge that I had accumulated over every step of my career into my new position because I was intentional about taking my time and learning.

I constantly tried to stay updated with the "latest and greatest" knowledge, rules, laws, strategic approaches, techniques, and tools that would help me to maximize my current career position, and this always helped me in the next one. I think that this is what really helped me win. I didn't rush. As a result, instead of me going and looking for a principal job, because of all that I had taken the time to learn throughout my career, the principal job came looking for me! In fact, while I was still an assistant principal, I was asked several times to become a principal. My answer was always "No. I don't know everything I need to know yet." It wasn't until I was finally ready that I said "Yes" to the principal position.

Therefore, one of my best pieces of advice to you is to never stop learning; get all of the knowledge you can from every career position you hold. Maximize it by pulling every bit of valuable information out of it that you possibly can. This is one of the most vital approaches that has contributed to my success as a transformational leader; it was something I did at 20 years old, and it was something I was still doing when I hit 40 years old. I've never changed it because it works!

The Final Outcome:
My Success = My Students' Success

In the end, my success was the students' success. Ninety-eight percent of the seniors that were on our campus this past year graduated and earned $3.7 million in scholarships. Are we saying that our work is done and that our mission is fully accomplished? Of course not. However, we are headed down the right path. If we continue in the direction of minimal dropouts, better attendance, increase test scores, one-on-one mentoring and monitoring, ensuring that every one of them completes a financial aid application and that each of them enrolls in either a full-time university, a two-year university, or the military, our school has no choice but to be one of the greatest neighborhood schools in Houston and the surrounding areas.

Leading this high school as a turnaround principal has been, by far, my most exciting time in education. I have experienced a young lady missing school in order to take care of her younger brother and sister every day, but after multiple conversations with her parents and a few bus cards, watching her return to school and graduate. More importantly, she was awarded $400,000 in scholarships and will be going off to attend Philander Smith College in Little Rock, Arkansas.

I've watched a young lady who thought she was done with school need a daily text sent every day, because getting her to come to school was a battle. We'd send her messages saying, "Are you awake?" "Are you on your way to school?" "I'm in your first period, and you're not here! Do we need to come get you?" In the beginning, she was late every single day, always missing her entire first period. However, after staying on top of her – relentlessly – she started coming to school on time, and would even stop somewhere on the way to school to pick up breakfast and bring it to us! She would arrive, cheerfully saying, "Hey! I'm on time, and I brought breakfast!" The transformation in her life was amazing to witness, and the only two ingredients that were missing from her recipe for success were accountability and love. She graduated from our school and she is now thriving. I've watched kids leave Sunnyside for the first time in their life on a plane with tears in their eyes because of the excitement and nervousness. I've watched them walk the campus of Georgetown University with eyes bright and wide, having never thought college, surely not out of state, was an option. I've watched kids with tears in their eyes walk across the stage as the first graduate in their family or with their kids in the audience cheering them on.

I count it a privilege to be the leader who cared enough to invest in the turnarounds and lead change in the schools. I know that in doing so, I changed the lives of students and forever altered the trajectory of their lives. Before I became a transformational leader, I had a desire to do this work. I was humbled by this work. I pose this question to you as you navigate your leadership pathway:

what are you currently doing in your work to create a posture of humbleness? After all, this work is truly servant leadership. It is my hope and prayer that by investing in the lives of those in your organization as a leader that you, too, will be able to turn around the lives of the students, who deserve the best of all that we have to offer them. When this happens, I encourage you to share your own story of success in order to help other educators who come after you make a difference by changing lives. People often glorify the position, not knowing the purpose or drive behind it. You must understand your why for the work you do and strive to do something bigger with what you have!

At the end of the day, always remember that whatever you're doing as a transformational leader, you're doing it for a bigger cause. In my case, we weren't just saving a school; we were saving the entire community that was wrapped around the school. Transforming the school in order to keep its doors open and give the kids, the school, and the community such a big win has been the most memorable event of my career, and an honor of a lifetime.

Chapter 7
Transformational Leadership Tips

TLT 7.1
Key 1: Toss the Traditional Job Description

- Operate through a different lens as you process your new role as a transformational leader. You are embarking upon some of the hardest work you'll ever encounter in your professional career. Do what is necessary and LEGAL to move the school forward. Be prepared to think outside of the box!

TLT 7.2
Key 2: Know How Your Grade and School Level Works

- Understand the operational context in which you are leading. It is imperative that you familiarize yourself with every aspect of the work and how each one functions.

TLT 7.3
Key 3: Know the System and Learn How to Work It

- Systems and processes may already be in place once you arrive on campus as the new leader. Internalize them, taking note of what works and capitalizing on them in order to use them to your advantage.

TLT 7.4
Key 4: Take the Time to Build Your Career and Learn as You Go

- Focus is key as you acquire the needed skillset to one day become a principal. Intentionally take the time to learn your position and be effective in it.

Endnotes

1 White, S. (2018, February). What is transformational leadership? A model for motivating innovation. *CIO Online* (from IDG). Retrieved from https://www.cio.com/article/3257184/leadership-management/what-is-transformational-leadership-a-model-for-motivating-innovation.html

2 Ibid.

3 Bass, B. (2010). Two decades of research and development in transformational leadership. *European Journal of Work and Organizational Psychology*, 8(1), 9-32. doi 10.1080/135943299398410

4 Bass, B., & Riggio, R. (2006). *Transformational leadership, 2nd ed*. Mahwah, NJ: Lawrence Erlbaum Associates.

5 Hein, R. (2013). How to apply transformational leadership at your company. *CIO Online* (from IDG). Retrieved from https://www.cio.com/article/2384791/careers-staffing/careers-staffing-how-to-apply-transformational-leadership-at-your-company.html

6 Bass, B. (2010). Two decades of research and development in transformational leadership.

7 White, S. (2018, February). What is transformational leadership?

8 Bass, B., & Riggio, R. (2006). *Transformational leadership*.

9 Bass, B. (2010). Two decades of research and development in transformational leadership.

10 Bass, B. (2010). Two decades of research and development in transformational leadership, p. 9

46042038R00118